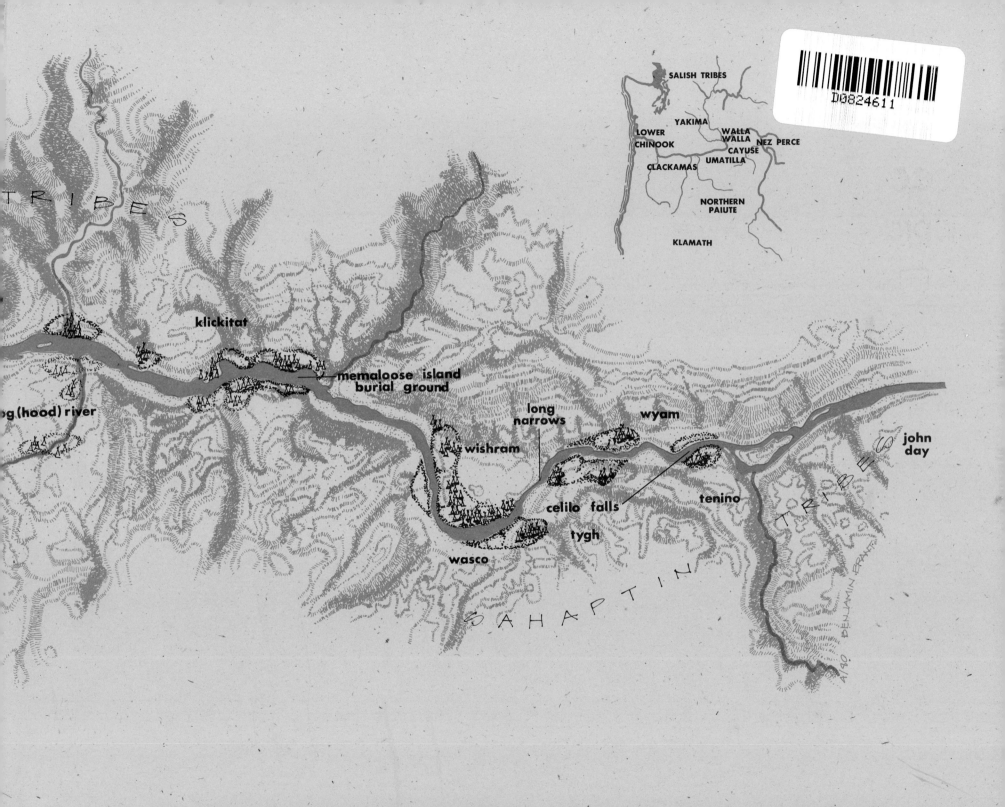

SALISH TRIBES

YAKIMA
LOWER
CHINOOK
WALLA
WALLA
NEZ PERCE
CAYUSE
CLACKAMAS
UMATILLA

NORTHERN
PAIUTE

KLAMATH

TRIBES

klickitat

memaloose island
burial ground

og (hood) river

long
narrows

wyam

wishram

john
day

celilo falls

tenino

tygh

wasco

SAHAPTIN TRIBES

BENJAMIN BRANT

Best wishes,

Chuck Williams

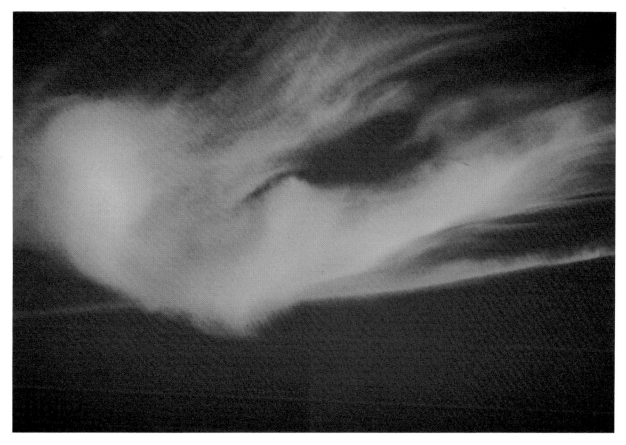

Sunset clouds from Larch Mountain.

Civilization is a thin veneer over what made us what we are.
—SIGURD OLSON[1]

Mount St. Helens (pre-eruption) from atop Silver Star.

Mount St. Helens erupting, March 1980.

From British Columbia to northern California the Cascade Range parallels the Pacific Ocean, hoarding the region's rains and creating an inland desert. Towering above the range are solitary cones, almost dormant volcanos. They are now sculpted by glaciers and streams, and draped with forests and alpine gardens, but periodically return to life.

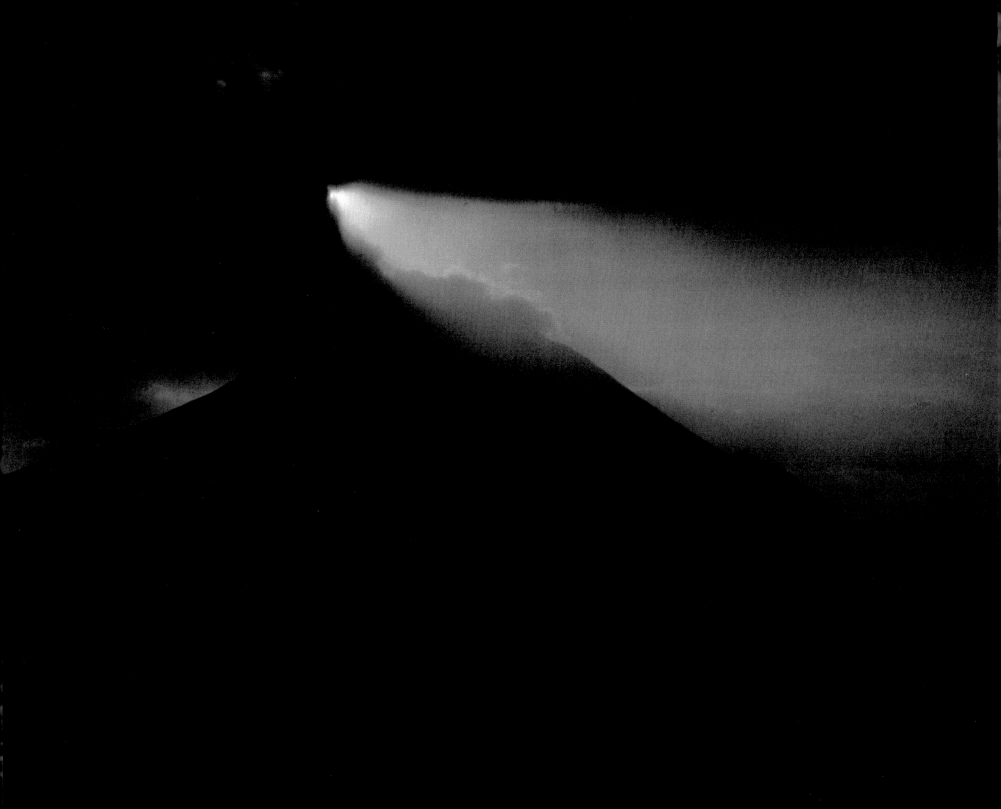

Most of the vast region between the Cascades and the Rocky Mountains drains into a single watershed, the Columbia, "The River of the West." It rises in the Canadian Rockies and wanders around the Northwest capturing such rivers as the Spokane and the Snake. The combined waters, aided by gravel and gravity, finally break through the Cascade Range between Mt. Adams and Mt. Hood, along what is now the Oregon–Washington border. The result of this meeting is a long and deep canyon, the Columbia Gorge, the only sea-level mixing of the two worlds normally separated by the mountain range.

Mount St. Helens erupting, March 1980.

The Columbia from the air.

Starvation Creek Falls received its name when a train full of passengers was stranded near the creek for three weeks by a fierce snowstorm in the winter of 1884-5; no one actually starved.

John Mix Stanley painted this romantic scene of the Columbia Gorge and Mt. Hood in 1871.

The west end of the Columbia Gorge is a lush rain forest of giant trees, ferns and waterfalls. Humidity reigns; the constant drizzle from clouds arriving from the ocean is occasionally broken by snow or harsh storms, or by a few days of drying sunshine. Thick vegetation clothes the land in green; only the lakes and rivers and volcanic cliffs remain exposed. Newborn sprouts responding to the constant watering receive nutrition from the moss-covered dead. Plants grow so fast and thick that travel is possible only by cutting a swath or by floating the river.

From Larch Mountain.

In the middle of the Gorge, east of the divide, the air suddenly turns drier, the land browner, the sky bluer. Cedar and Douglas fir thin into ponderosa pine. The rain forest dissolves in the sunlight, leaving oaks and grasslands reminiscent of California's hills, complete with orange poppies and poison oak.

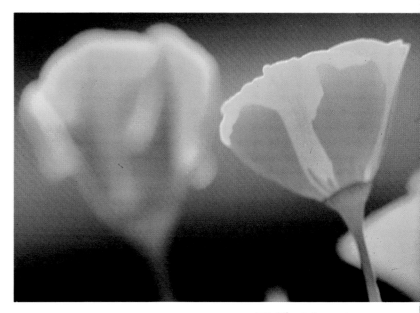

"California" poppies.

Across from Mitchell Point, which
natives thought parted storms.

9

The Columbia from east of Mosier.

Further east in the Gorge this transitional landscape blends into the sagebrush and sand dunes of the "cold desert" created by the barrier of the Cascade Mountains. The wind blows harder, and the twists and contortions of the earth itself are again exposed.

Sand dunes east of The Dalles.

One of the largest Cascade Indian villages was located on the river bank west of Beacon Rock.

Fishing Columbia River

*"Below the Cascades" was painted
by Paul Kane in 1847.*

Once upon a time the Columbia River was filled with salmon, the buffalo of the Northwest, and the Gorge's cascades and waterfalls made for good fishing. Before the coming of the white people and their diseases and dams, salmon supported an exceptionally large Native American population. Village after village lined the great river.

Just as it is the meeting ground of the wet ocean weather and the more extreme dry continental climate, the Gorge was the gathering place for many diverse Indian tribes and the transition between the canoe people of the rainy western slope and the foot and horse cultures of the arid plateaus to the east.

I am descended both from the almost–extinct Native American tribe that lived at the west end of the Columbia Gorge and from the European pioneers that replaced them and immediately began remodeling.

This is our story...

My great-grandmother, Kalliah, best-known as "Indian Mary."

The view from Kalliah's cabin site.

Once in his life a man ought to concentrate his mind upon the remembered earth, I believe. He ought to give himself up to a particular landscape in his experience, to look at it from as many angles as he can, to wonder about it, to dwell upon it. He ought to imagine that he touches it with his hands at every season and listens to the sounds that are made upon it. He ought to imagine the creatures there and all the faintest motions of the wind. He ought to recollect the glare of noon and all the colors of the dawn and dusk.

—N. Scott Momaday[2]

Near Viento (Windy).

The Oregon escarpment from Indian Mary Road near Skamania.

This book is dedicated to
two life–long friends
born and raised in
the Columbia Gorge:
my father,
A. Clyde Williams,
and the late
Stella Walker Hazard,
my neighbor across the creek.

ISBN: 0-913890-43-X

Library of Congress
Catalog Card No. 80-52782

Printed in the U.S.A. by
Graphic Arts Center,
Portland, Oregon.

Multnomah Falls.

BRIDGE OF THE GODS, MOUNTAINS OF FIRE

A Return to the Columbia Gorge

text and photographs by *Chuck Williams*

introduction by *David R. Brower*

published by

FRIENDS OF THE EARTH ELEPHANT MOUNTAIN ARTS

NEW YORK · SAN FRANCISCO   WHITE SALMON · PETALUMA

in cooperation with the

COLUMBIA GORGE ENVIRONMENTAL CENTER
HOOD RIVER

In memory of
Emory Strong
and Justice
William O. Douglas,
two men who
loved the Gorge.

SPECIAL THANKS TO: Bettye Williams (my mom); Dave Brower, Greg, Bruce and Friends of the Earth Foundation; Doug Pfeiffer and the staff of Graphic Arts Center; David Gancher; the National Park Service; Columbia Gorge Ranger Station (U.S. Forest Service); the staff of the Columbia Gorge Commissions; Marsha, Val, Cliff and my other relatives; Ed Edmo; Don Lowe; Art Wolfe; Ruth Strong, Ivan Donaldson, Sharon Tiffany and the Skamania County Historical Society; Maryhill; Tom Vaughn, Susan Seyl and the staff of the Oregon Historical Society; Dennis and Bonnie White; Barbara Klinger; Ben Brant; Dannelle Pfeiffer; Maggie McLaughlin; John Yeon; Nancy Russell; Russ Jolley and OEC; WEC; Jeff Zucker; Craig Collins; Steve Yates; Barbara O'Neill; Friends of the White Salmon River; Mid-Columbia Concerned Citizens; Bruce; Audubon and the Cady's; the Wyers; Carroll; Kate; Vera; the Baumans; Les; the Schmidts; Del; John; Chris; Mike; Donald and Elizabeth Lawrence; David and Kathrine French; and all the other kind people who helped.

Horsetail Falls.

Contents

Introduction

Americans have developed an unusual skill in making one place look as usual as another, but we do not need that skill in the Columbia Gorge. The homogenization of America is too well under way already. A frequent traveler wonders which city's Holiday Inn he is in, or which former city's shopping center, and he can thank car license plates for telling him what state he is in. Level or rolling agricultural land, from one coast to another, becomes a commonplace when it is inundated by Xeroxed suburbia. City centers buy their high-rise boxes from the same salesman, right out of the catalog.

The challenge to proliferate mediocrity is a harder one when there is a mountain to be reduced, but never underestimate the power of the Chimera of Mindless Growth. Developers under its spell can level mountains, and they have. Canyons, especially deep ones, take a little longer. Be grateful that we still have the grand canyon of the Columbia where it breaks through the Cascades on its final dash to the sea. The developers, however, are closing in on it, from the ends, the sides, and from its very heart, the river. Is there an alternative approach? Can we, without alarming the people who still believe that unselective growth is progress, please people who love the Gorge for what it is and not what they can do to it?

An America as beautiful as this one once was can have much of its beauty restored in our own lifetimes. To make it so is a laudable national goal. The goal derives from a land ethic that needs to be rediscovered from time to time. Its base is our knowledge that however well buttressed in print or in mutual consent our title to a piece of land may seem, we are only brief tenants on it. We are privileged to enjoy the good things on that land left there by predecessors who treated it as if they trusted us to love it as they did. We are also doomed to suffer the harm thoughtlessly done to some places that cannot be healed in our time, if ever.

We can be grateful for the variety of ways that ingenious people have created to save for themselves and their descendants those special places where what counts is the miraculous interplay of the wild living things that were there and still are because they have been thoughtfully spared. In humanity's earliest days, places were saved because we did not yet have the tools to spoil them with. Later, when the tools had arrived — fire, the first of them — places were saved by taboo, or set aside for worship, or for princes to hunt in or people to be laid to rest in. Some places, of course, were spared by their remoteness or by the hazards that lay within them or were imagined to be there. Finally, places were saved by the will to share the earth with other living things than ourselves, including the largest human population of all—the people who have yet to arrive on the planet, but whose genes are here now, in our custody. It is fair to remember when we were in their predicament, and to conclude that they will one day be every bit as real as we are, and fully as critical of mistakes predecessors make.

Among the devices that is now saving great places, a device born of dreams, is the national park idea. It was born when Yosemite became the first park set aside for its beauty in legislation signed by Abraham Lincoln in 1864. The nation was not yet ready to administer Yosemite Valley and the Mariposa Grove of Big Trees. The task was assigned to the State of California but given back to the federal government in 1905, to be included in the surrounding Yosemite National Park, which had been established in 1890, eighteen years after Yellowstone. These dates and names are of fading importance in themselves, but they are important to what happens to the Columbia Gorge because it is time for a concept to grow anew.

In 1948 the *Sierra Club Bulletin* published an extraordinary article by Dr. Hans Huth entitled, "Yosemite: The Story of an Idea." He later expanded on the subject in his book, *Nature and the American* (University of California Press, 1957). Dr. Huth was not ready to accept the notion that the national park concept could have been born at Yellowstone. He traced it back to early cemeteries, planned for the living as well as the dead, convenient and pleasant places to visit. They would not be unlike the commons in early American cities. In 1836 William Cullen Bryant began advocating a public park in New York. Fifteen years later an act was passed enabling necessary lands to be purchased; Frederick Law Olmsted was appointed superintendent of the park project and Central Park took shape. Twelve years later still, having had a disagreement with New York park authorities, he accepted a position in California, where abuse of natural scenery was leading to protest. In the *Atlantic Monthly* in 1857, James Russell Lowell was advocating a society for the prevention of cruelty to trees. The next year *Harper's Weekly* lamented the destruction of one of the Calaveras Big Trees, which had been "peeled with as much neatness and industry as a troupe of jackals would display in clearing the bones of a dead lion." Yosemite had been discovered by White Man in 1833, but was not entered until 1851. Thomas

A. Ayres sketched the valley in 1855 and 1856; his sketches were lithographed and distributed widely in the East. The valley's scenery was called "perhaps the most remarkable in the United States, and perhaps in the world." Olmsted tried to work for its conservation. As Huth notes, "Certainly no one was better prepared to take an active part in urging the Yosemite grant and to keep the ball rolling." Roll it did. Senator John Conness introduced the Yosemite bill March 28, 1864, and President Lincoln signed it June 29. There were giants in those days.

Although the Yosemite legislation's wording is not notably cognizant of the national park idea, Olmsted was. In a long-lost report to the California legislature he stated that the first requirement is to preserve the natural scenery and restrict within the narrowest limits the necessary accommodation of visitors. Structures should not detract from the dignity of the scene. "In permitting the sacrifice of anything that would be of the slightest value to future visitors," he wrote, "to the convenience, bad taste, playfulness, carelessness, or wanton destructiveness of present visitors, we probably yield in each case the interest of uncounted millions to the selfishness of a few." He was certainly one of the first to be looking out for the greatest good for the greatest number in the long run, with emphasis on where it was needed and so often overlooked—that long run.

How long so far? Bryant wanting a public park in New York in 1836. New York beginning to get one in 1851. The nation getting one, in Yosemite, under state jurisdiction, in 1864; under federal jurisdiction in 1872 in Yellowstone. Yosemite and Sequoia national parks initiated in 1890 but not yet completed. A renaissance of Thoreau's belief in wildness and Muir's in wilderness through the good work of Aldo Leopold, Robert Marshall, and Howard Zahniser, culminating in the National Wilderness Preservation System enacted by the Congress, with a lone dissenting vote from Texas, in 1964, a century after Yosemite. Then the development in local communities of the zoning idea, by which land that had been protected by private owners who loved it, at their own expense, could be zoned to remain unspoiled, still at the owner's expense, while the unloving developed the land around them, often destructively and at handsome profit. More recently, the concept of land rights as a package of differing rights, that could be treated separately, so that development rights could be transferred, even air rights, without selling the land itself; scenic easements, too. Pleasuring places for people, sanctuaries for wildlife, then for plants, and, still more recently, the growing need for sanctuaries for people, where they could

be spared the sight and sound and smell of automobiles and pavement in the hot sun.

The national park idea spread around the world. Many nations, however, did not have the options of the U.S.; their wilderness had already nearly vanished. In Japan and many European countries, the national park concept evolved to include mixed public and private lands, with a continuation of compatible uses, such as farming. Now the U.S., by necessity, must look to these variations of an idea born at Yosemite and Yellowstone. A start has been made. Farming and grazing are part of the newer national recreation areas, and President John F. Kennedy, with Cape Cod National Seashore in 1962, expanded the National Park System to include scenic communities. In 1978 Congress authorized a prototype "greenline park," Pinelands National Reserve, to protect New Jersey's million-acre Pine Barrens with a minimum of federal acquisition. These new parklands are not a panacea, however, and are definitely not a substitute for the traditional wilderness parks. The bitter controversies that surround Adirondack State Park, a huge area in New York that mixes publicly-owned wilderness with private lands regulated by a commission, show how difficult the path will be.

In a sense, Olmsted and friends had it easy. Their world was an empty one, with just a fraction of today's population. Even so, it took decades, sometimes a century and more, for their ideas to be reflected in a place.

Chuck Williams has not had it that easy, nor do we. To give the Columbia Gorge a fair chance, in the long run, is going to require a combining of all the best ideas there have been to guide humanity in its use of a place the beauty of which is too great to squander, and now far too rare. The Gorge was still almost a wilderness when John Muir visited it and marveled at its beauty. It would have been an outstanding national park, but "progress" has blocked that option. Instead, if protected in a national scenic area as proposed by Friends of the Earth and local conservationists, the Columbia Gorge will be a milestone in scenic and historic preservation, a creative mixture of public and private lands —and an important precedent for the second century of the national park concept.

Chuck Williams has a lot of Ayres in him in his artistry, much of Olmsted in his deep knowledge of parks, and no little giant in him. Hear him out. Share his love, if you will, of a great place. And joining his with your own ideas and energy, come to the rescue!

July 8, 1980

DAVID R. BROWER, *Founder*
Friends of the Earth

1. *Bridge of the Gods*

*It is always worthwhile to sit or kneel
at the feet of grandeur, to look up
into the placid faces of the earth gods
and feel their power.*

—JOHN BURROUGHS[3]

The sun was totally eclipsed over the Gorge in 1979.

*"Sunset on the Columbia" was painted
by James Everett Stuart in 1929.*

Skamania and Beacon Rock from Cape Horn.

The Columbia Gorge is the mystic center of my childhood memories. My parents emigrated to northern California looking for work when I was young, but we returned often to the Northwest. The high points of the trips, besides visiting the generous uncle that owned a model airplane factory in Portland, were the excursions to the family land in the Columbia Gorge.

Leaving Portland we crossed the Columbia River and followed it east with Mt. Hood sometimes visible atop the horizon. After visiting relatives that lived within the stench of the Camas pulp mill, we left the flat bottomlands and wound up a mountain, the west slope of the Cascades, until we lost sight of the river.

Suddenly the road crested over Cape Horn, one of the Gorge's portals; and we would find ourselves on the lip of a giant abyss. The west end of the Columbia Gorge, the deep green canyon we were entering, was another world: the world of my ancestors. If it wasn't cloudy, Beacon Rock marked our way as it did Lewis and Clark's. Just beyond it, where the canyon pinched in and the rapids used to be, was the site of the legendary Bridge of the Gods that Indian stories claim once spanned the Columbia River.

Following the road as it hugged the lichen-decorated cliff face, through a covered bridge intended to protect cars from falling rocks, we dropped into the Gorge. Down in this chasm, at a place known as Skamania, was the family land: my father's heritage. He was born on this land, in the back of the old general store which my grandparents used to run. It has long since disappeared into the jungle, and I now live about a hundred feet away from its site. I am named for this grandfather, a Welch-English-Scotch settler and jack-of-all-trades, and bear an uncanny resemblance to him. My grandmother, one of the last full-blooded Cascade Indians, was also raised on this land; and her mother, Kalliah, well-known as "Indian Mary," lived here after the hanging of her father, Tumalth, a village chief who lived a few miles upriver where Bonneville Dam now is.

My ancestors and the other Native Americans of the Columbia Gorge were humbled by its giant trees and waterfalls and canyon walls. Like peoples everywhere, they explained to themselves why certain things happened and what became of humans after they were no longer living. Earth was their mother, Sun their father. They believed in a supreme being, although the concept of *Tyhee Sahale,* the Great Spirit, was probably in part a creation of the early Christian missionaries. Living close to the elements these people often felt ignored, even victimized, by their deities. Help was sometimes needed from animals to persuade, or even trick, some of these gods. The Great Spirit was often elsewhere when needed and so left the people at the dubious mercy of less-benevolent demigods, including volcanoes and the monstrous Thunderbird, *Tatoosh,* who brought terrible storms from the ocean, shot lightning from his single eye and ate whales for snacks.

My Indian ancestors believed that animals and even trees and other plants had souls, could be communicated with and had to be treated with respect to ensure their cooperation. Even rocks had feelings. Evil spirits, sometimes in the form of monsters, hid at such places as Celilo Falls and the Great Cascades to eat canoeists who thought portaging unnecessary. Some animals had god-like powers, although they often abused their special gifts. Many stories of their exploits have come down my family tree.4

Lower Multnomah Falls.

Mount St Helens with smoke from the crater hovering in a peculiar form over the top of the mountain

Paul Kane painted Mount St. Helens venting steam in 1847.

Long, long ago, when the world was very young and people hadn't come out yet, Earth was inhabited by huge animal–people who hunted, fished, dug roots, lived in houses, married, made many mistakes and generally lived as humans later did. These animal–people were huge; Mosquito and Spider, for example, were bigger than cows are now.

Foremost among these animal demigods was Coyote the Trickster. Coyote was brilliant, "the smartest of animals," and possessed magical powers given him by the Great Spirit as a reward for helping the people. Usually Coyote was well-meaning, but he also had a mischievous streak that often led to trouble. Coyote helped prepare Earth for the people and stole fire for them from a volcano. His shortcomings, especially his self-indulgences, were not unlike human frailties; and his insatiable sexual appetite often got him into trouble.

Other animals that the Indians considered cunning, especially Fox and Raven, played similar roles. The animals necessary to the survival of the people — such as Salmon and Elk — were treated with deep reverence, as were the deceased, who could return at night as ghosts. Coyote even brought permanent death into the world. Had it not been for his Orphean impatience to get his wife back from the Land of the Dead (he looked at her before he was supposed to), the deceased could have returned every spring with the flowers.

When the first people came to live by *Wauna,* the Columbia River, they did not have mouths; their faces were smooth between their noses and chins. The men hunted and fished; the women picked berries and dug roots. They were good cooks, but they could not eat. They could be fed only by smelling food, and so they developed an acute sense of smell. But they were happy — although they sometimes talked with each other in sign language about how all of the other animals on Earth had mouths.

One day Coyote came up the river and saw that the people had no mouths. This made him sad because he knew that this was not part of the Great Spirit's plan. The Great Spirit had to create all plants and animals before people so that the humans would have things to eat — and must have overlooked their mouths in the rush to finish creation. Coyote offered to cut mouths for the people, but they were reluctant, fearing that he would botch the job and leave them worse off. Finally Coyote convinced them by showing how he could eat and sing and talk with the animals.

Coyote gathered the people far up the Deschutes River at the base of Mt. Multnomah, a volcano that has since disappeared. On Coyote's instructions, the men collected firewood and built a huge fire at the base of the black cliffs. Then the women threw on cold water that shattered the rocks into many tiny blades. Pieces of chert you find now that have dull edges were the knives Coyote used to cut mouths.

Coyote had the people lie down, grouped by families and tribes; then he put them to sleep. At first he just cut straight lines, but as he studied their faces, Coyote decided to cut their mouths so that their hearts could be read on their faces. It took him many days to cut all of the mouths, and when he was tired, he didn't always do a good job. Sometimes he was so exhausted that he leaned on peoples' noses and flattened them. When Coyote was done, he awoke the people and warned them not to eat or talk until their mouths had healed. But some were too impatient to wait, so the corners of their mouths drooped down when they tried to talk.

The people were even happier with mouths and soon learned to talk to each other and to the animals. Now that the people were able to eat, they could store food for the winter when the Spirit of the Cold came down from the north and drove away Sun, which gave their food strong odors. The people elected Coyote as their spokesman to the Great Spirit, who rewarded him by granting the power to change into any form and back again.

Back when Coyote came up the river and cut mouths for the people, most of them lived on the shores of a great inland sea east of the Cascade Range. Fish, birds, game, berries and roots were plentiful, and Coyote gave the people the Law so that they could live together in peace.

On the western side of the great sea lived two sons of the Great Spirit: Wy-east (Mt. Hood) and Pah-toe (Mt. Adams). The Great Spirit had shot two arrows into the air — one to the north of the Columbia, the other to the south — and told the brothers to settle where the arrows landed. After many years of living together happily, a beautiful woman mountain moved into the valley between the brothers. She fell in love with Wy-east, the smaller mountain-god, but liked to make him jealous by flirting with good-natured Pah-toe. Soon both brothers fell madly in love with her and began to quarrel with each other over matters of little importance. At first they only growled at each other and stamped their feet, shaking the ground. Coyote tried to reason with the once-close brothers, but to no avail. The brothers then threw fire and rocks at each other, and the black smoke from their terrifying battle hid Sun, bringing darkness to Earth.

Finally they stopped to rest. When the smoke cleared away, their beautiful white coats had disappeared — and the landscape was devastated. The forest and the plants the people ate had burned; the animals had fled or been killed. The villages were also burned, and the people had fled or hid in caves. Worst of all, the brothers had shaken the ground so hard that a hole was broken through the mountain range between them. The great inland sea escaped through the hole, and the torrent enlarged it into a huge tunnel. During the darkness, the Beautiful Woman Mountain had hidden in a cave.

Coyote fetched the Great Spirit, who arrived just in time to stop the brothers from fighting again, this time over who was to blame for the disappearance of the woman mountain they had been so noisily courting. The Great Spirit was furious with them and decreed that the Beautiful Woman Mountain would remain hidden in the cave. He left the natural bridge that spanned what had become a huge river as a symbol of peace and so that the humans and the animals could still visit each other easily. The Great Spirit warned that if the brothers ever fought again, the Bridge of the Gods would be destroyed and the brothers forever separated. He also placed an old woman mountain, Loo-wit (Mount St. Helens), the keeper of the fire, by the bridge to guard it and remind the brothers of how transitory youthful beauty is.

Slowly the people returned to their homes, but there were only mud flats where the inland sea had been. Ash covered everything, making breathing difficult. The people were on the edge of starvation, so they looked for Coyote to help. When Coyote came up the river, they blamed him for their troubles. Coyote became angry and threatened to remove their mouths and to return them to their original condition. Like most people, however, they wanted to keep their blessings while blaming those who had blessed them. They finally apologized to Coyote.

The only solution, Coyote said, was to journey down the river to the sea and bring fish back to feed the people. Coyote chose six of the ablest men, and they set off in the best war-canoe, not knowing what to expect. When they approached the Bridge of the Gods, Coyote, who was sitting in the prow of the canoe, gave them a last chance to back out. They were all afraid of what evil spirits might await them in that dark tunnel, but they did not want to show fear before Coyote. The river, too, evidently was scared; it sped up as it entered the hole in the mountains.

No sooner had the group entered total darkness than the canoe crashed into an island, and they were thrown onto a pile of driftwood. The canoe was safe, but the paddles, their provisions and one man were gone. Coyote was still with them, though. He took a fire starter from his hair and started a fire on the island. Soon the men were warm and new paddles were carved from driftwood.

The group swept on downstream aided by the light from the big fire. The tunnel was so large that they couldn't see the top. They could barely see one shoreline, where they found their missing companion clinging to a piece of driftwood. When he climbed into the canoe, it began to fill with water from a hole incurred in the wreck. Coyote came to the rescue again; he changed into a beaver and towed the canoe out of the tunnel and into the welcome sunlight so it could be patched.

The devastation was even worse on the west side of the Cascades. The Multnomah (Willamette) River had already carved a narrow course to the sea, but it could not accommodate the floodwaters of the Columbia; another inland sea had formed. The canoe drifted as darkness set in, and the men, exhausted from their ordeal, fell asleep. They awoke at dawn to find themselves being swept into the great salt sea. They landed, and Coyote built a fire to warm them. They saw smoke rising far to the north; thinking it a village where food could be obtained, the men walked up the beach, which was covered with dead fish, trees, canoes and even parts of houses from their homeland.

Too exhausted to take normal precautions, they were captured by hostile villagers and taken prisoners. Even Coyote was too weary to use his special powers; this shook the faith of his companions, but they were too tired to think about it very much. But when the men were brought before the village chief, he jumped to his feet and embraced Coyote. It seems that Coyote in his distant travels had once saved this chief from a giant bear, so the exhausted men were freed; they feasted on salmon, clams, cranberries, venison and roots until they fell asleep.

When they awoke the next morning, they again saw many dead fish floating in the salt water. Their new friend, the chief, offered some of his salmon since they could also live in fresh water. Enough salmon were rounded up to fill the river from bank to bank and, with the help of seagulls and sea-dogs (seals), they were driven upstream through the Bridge of the Gods to the starving people. On the advice of the Great Spirit, Coyote and the people escorted salmon up the river twice a year until the salmon learned the way; after five years, the salmon came upriver on their own.5 Happiness returned.

"Mount St. Helens erupting" by Paul Kane, 1847.

Mt. Hood from Tanner Butte.

It was again peaceful on Earth for many years, and the scars of the battle healed. But the Beautiful Woman Mountain got lonely in her cave; everyone was living a good life, but she was not allowed to join them. The Great Spirit had sent a tribe of beautiful birds, the Bats, to keep her company and to bring her news from the outside — and to make sure she didn't leave the cave. She was so beautiful and good-hearted that the Bats, too, came to love her. They pleaded for her freedom, but the Great Spirit was afraid that her appearance above ground would cause another major battle.

Wy-east, who was ashamed of the damage caused by his jealousy, found out that the Bats were her guardians; and through them, he began secret correspondence with the Beautiful Woman Mountain. Together, they finally persuaded the Bats to let her slip out at night — for some healthy, fresh air. Wy-east played on the sympathies of Loo-wit, the elderly guardian of the Bridge of the Gods; and she allowed him to sneak across the bridge at night to see his loved one.

The couple met happily for many moons, but—as lovers so often do—one night they stayed too long. Wy-east ran back to the bridge as it was getting light, but he was so gigantic that he shook Earth; a huge boulder fell and blocked his lover's cave. The Sun came up, and the Great Spirit caught the lovers. He was furious, but mainly with the Bats since the Beautiful Woman Mountain had only done what anyone would have in her situation. He punished the Bats by transforming them into an ugly combination of bird and beast and decreed that they would forever have to spend their days hanging upside down from the roofs of caves and could go out only at night.

The Great Spirit allowed the Beautiful Woman Mountain to remain outside her cave, and the lovers requested permission to marry; but the Great Spirit was afraid that their marriage would spark another battle between the brothers. She was very discreet and dressed only in dull colors, but she still seemed to excite the brothers. They were held back by the Great Spirit who promised to find a mate for Pah-toe, but with all of the work it never got done.

Then one day when the Great Spirit was away from the Earth, the brothers suddenly threw off their white robes and began another terrifying fight. They threw rocks and liquid fire at each other and shook the Earth so hard that the Bridge of the Gods fell into the river. Many of the rocks they threw fell short and squeezed the river, forming the Narrows. Ignoring the pleas of their friends, the brothers fought until Pah-toe, who was larger, finally won. The Beautiful Woman Mountain dutifully took her place next to Pah-toe (Mt. Adams), but she was so heartbroken because she loved Wy-east (Mt. Hood) that she fell into a deep sleep. She can still be seen in her drab clothes next to Pah-toe; she is now called Sleeping Beauty. Once, Pah-toe held his head high as Wy-east still does, but when he saw what happened to the mountain he loved, he dropped his head in sadness.

Loo-wit, the elderly mountain, had valiantly tried to stop the war and to protect the Bridge of the Gods; but she was badly battered and fell into the river with the arch. When the Great Spirit finally arrived, it was too late to stop the disaster. But hearing Loo-wit's moans, the Great Spirit decided to reward her bravery by giving her one wish. She replied that she would like to be young and beautiful again. The Great Spirit smiled and replied that while she could become physically young again, her memory and her mind could not be altered. She replied that she preferred it that way, so her wish was granted. Since her old friends and relatives had passed on and she was content by herself, aloof Loo-wit (Mt. St. Helens) moved west, away from the other mountains. She can still be seen today, the youngest-looking and most beautiful of the snow mountains; but some people claim she is restless.

Mount St. Helens on May 18, 1980, the day she blew her top.

Below Kalliah's cabin site near Skamania.

In the course of these battles, all the plants had been burned, the animals had been driven away—and the fallen Bridge of the Gods had formed a huge dam that flooded the Gorge for a great distance to the east, blocking the salmon runs. With the help of East Wind, the people again fetched Coyote, who had married the daughter of the friendly chief at the great salt sea. Coyote came up the river and changed himself into a gigantic dog. With his paws he dug a channel through the new dam so the salmon could again return upriver to feed the people. The rapids he created in the process were later known as the Great Cascades of the Columbia and became a famous fishing site.

Coyote then headed east, but was so tired that he forgot to return to his original form. He approached two young Indian women who were as beautiful as a spring morning with dew on the opening blossoms; they were singing with voices as soft and lovely as that of *Wauna,* the great river herself. Seeing the monstrous dog, the women fled. Coyote chased and finally caught them. He tried to talk to them, but they were too scared; in weary anger, Coyote changed them to stone. They can be seen near the mouth of Fifteenmile Creek, east of The Dalles. A brave chief, Waubash, the lover of one of the women, then attacked giant Coyote, but he was thrown against the cliff across from Hood River, where he can still be seen.

The Great Spirit finally returned and was appalled by the sight of the devastated landscape. He was also furious with Coyote for violently losing his temper twice in one day and punished the demigod by making him forever retain the form of a small dog. But in gratitude for the good that Coyote had done, the Great Spirit let him keep his cunning brain so that he could survive difficult situations. Coyote could return to his original form only on rare occasions, which occurred on full moons. Peace returned, at least for awhile, and the people were again happy.

With these legends in our minds, my sister and I searched for arrowheads and fishing weights; the family land remained wild enough that we could pick berries and catch fish and talk to bears. Little imagination was needed to step back in time.

Salmonberry.

Berry vines near Kalliah's cabin site.

2. Fire and Rain

Oregon as it is to-day is a very young country, though most of it seems old. Contemplating the Columbia sweeping from forest to forest, across plain and desert, one is led to say of it as did Byron of the ocean, "Such as Creation's dawn beheld, thou rollest now." How ancient appear the crumbling basalt monuments along its banks, and the gray plains to the east of the Cascades! Nevertheless, the river as well as its basin in anything like the present condition are comparatively but of yesterday. Looking no further back in the geological records than the tertiary period, the Oregon of that time looks altogether strange in the few suggestive glimpses we may get of it — forests in which palm trees wave their royal crowns, and strange animals roaming beneath them or about the reedy margins of lakes, the Oreodon, Lephiodon, and several extinct species of the horse, the camel, and other animals.

Then came the fire period with its darkening showers of ashes and cinders and its vast floods of molten lava, making quite another Oregon from the fair and fertile land of the preceding era. And again while yet the volcanic fires show signs of action in the smoke and flame of the higher mountains, the whole region passes under the dominion of ice, and from the frost and darkness and death of the Glacial Period, Oregon has but recently emerged to the kindly warmth and life of to-day.

—John Muir[6]

Most geologists doubt that a Bridge of the Gods with a huge tunnel beneath it ever existed, but about 700 years ago a major slide did block the river at the site of the legendary arch and created the Great Cascades of the Columbia. Now covered by the reservoir behind Bonneville Dam, the Great Cascades were once rapids that would make any modern river-runner drool. Most early boaters, however, detested the impassable "white-water."

1855 railroad survey illustration of the Cascades.

David Douglas, the botanist who named the Cascade Mountains for these rapids, wrote in March 1826:

The scenery at this season is likewise grand beyond description; the high mountains in the neighborhood, which are covered with pines of several species, some of which grow to an enormous size, are all loaded with snow; the rainbow from the vapour of the agitated water, which rushes with furious rapidity over shattered rocks and through deep caverns producing an agreeable although at the same time somewhat melancholy echo through the thick wooded valley; the reflections from the snow on the mountains, together with the vivid green of the gigantic pines, form a contrast of rural grandeur that can scarcely be surpassed.

Niagara Falls was then considered the standard for scenic wonders. Thomas Farnham wrote that "the Cascades must present a spectacle of sublimity equalled only by Niagara," and missionary Samuel Parker, visiting the Gorge in 1836, added:

Each time the scenery of these Cascades is beheld, new wonders unfold themselves. Niagara itself, if we expect its unbroken fall of one hundred and fifty feet, cannot bear a comparison with the superior style of natures work here.

The massive slide that formed the Great Cascades is a relatively recent happening in the geologic history of the Columbia Gorge; millions of years were first needed to create the mountains and cut the water gap.

Oneonta Gorge.

After the Northwest emerged from shallow seas, but before the Cascade Mountains rose, the Columbia River flowed across a wide valley south of where the Gorge later formed. About thirty million years ago, heavy rains eroded loose ash from ancient volcanoes, forming thin mudflows that carried volcanic rocks over much of the region. This Miocene layer of the earth's surface, called the Eagle Creek Formation, is visible along the side canyons cut by Eagle, Tanner and Moffett Creeks; it contains petrified logs and leaf prints of extinct trees.[7]

Covering the Eagle Creek mudflows are layers of Columbia River (Yakima) Basalt, or Coriba, the thickest formation and the backdrop of most of the Gorge's waterfalls. These Miocene exudations flowed about twenty million years ago, primarily from northeast Oregon; the molten basalt covered 250,000 square miles of the Columbia Basin to depths of two thousand feet. When the basalt cooled, it often cracked into pentagonal columns that adorn many of the Gorge's steep walls. Since this formation thins to the south, below Mt. Hood, and to the north, where it is visible at high elevations near Hamilton Mountain, it evidently filled a wide valley. The Columbia was forced northward but continued to cross the emerging mountain range by cutting a channel through the successive layers of basalt. Enough time lapsed between basalt flows for soil to form and trees to grow; casts of these trees can be seen as holes in the lava cliffs of Oneonta Gorge.

Overlying the thick Columbia River Basalt are Pliocene sediments evidently deposited by the Columbia River. These sandstone layers are imbedded with rocks and pebbles and are usually called the Troutdale Formation in the western end of the Gorge, the Rhododendron Formation between Tanner and Herman Creeks, and the Dalles Formation to the east. Quartzite pebbles swept down from British Columbia are common in this formation near the present river.[8]

The interweaving of these formations indicates that the uplifting of the Cascade Range had begun by this time, a process that continued for millions of years. The Columbia, however, unlike many other Northwest rivers, was able to carve a channel fast enough to maintain a westward course. A huge arch rose up thousands of feet between faults in the Portland Basin and the Hood River Valley,[9] allowing the river to cut down into the rising Eagle Creek Formation. The Columbia's flow increased greatly during the Cascade Range's fastest uplifting, and the swift and full river carved through the rock so fast that in the Gorge the tributaries were left hanging above, forming waterfalls.

Basalt cliffs west of Dallesport. East of Hood River, the earth buckled, forming the undulations (anticlines and synclines) that are so vivid in the arid end of the Gorge.

Mount St. Helens on "Ash Sunday." The plume on the left was probably steam from a boiling Spirit Lake.

During the last few million years, the final geologic toppings, the Cascade and Boring lava flows, were deposited by the extinct volcanoes, such as Larch Mountain and Underwood Mountain, that line the Gorge. This magma also flowed from dikes that pushed up through older layers and then cooled and hardened to form spectacular monoliths such as Beacon Rock.

Growing volcanoes, such as Mt. Adams and Mt. Hood, erupted on both sides of the Gorge and sent recent molten flows down the Little White Salmon Valley and Hood River Valley. Early pioneers saw Mount St. Helens erupt numerous times between 1842 and 1857, and explorer John Fremont reported an eruption that dumped half an inch of ash on The Dalles. Loo-wit remained quiet, however, from 1857 until early in 1980, when new eruptions shook the area and dumped ash on the Gorge and across the country, a reminder that geology is not limited to the ancient past.

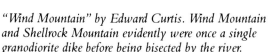

Mount St. Helens seen from the air.

"Wind Mountain" by Edward Curtis. Wind Mountain and Shellrock Mountain evidently were once a single granodiorite dike before being bisected by the river.

Ice flows on the Sandy River.

The continental ice sheets did not extend as far south as the Gorge during the Wisconsin Ice Age, but glaciers flowed down from the highest peaks, including down the Hood River Valley and the Sandy River Canyon almost to the Columbia River. Near the end of this Ice Age, more than ten thousand years ago, a great deluge swept through the Gorge, only the most recent of many such floods. Ice flows blocked the Clark Fork of the Columbia River and backed up over what is now Idaho and Montana enough water to half fill Lake Michigan. Suddenly this ice dam burst, quickly draining the inland sea. This torrent of water, thought to be ten times the combined flow of all the world's rivers, scoured eastern Washington, stripping wide areas of soil down to bedrock and creating the Channeled Scablands. The rampaging sea entered the narrow course of the Columbia at Wallula Gap, and the narrow constriction temporarily created another inland lake. This deluge, known as the Missoula (or Bretz or Spokane) Flood, filled the Gorge to above Crown Point, leaving boulders carried in icebergs a thousand feet above The Dalles, and spilled over Fifteenmile Creek and the high gap between Chanticleer and Crown Points. These floods widened the Gorge and flushed away much of the soft Eagle Creek Formation that surrounded the volcanic plug now known as Beacon Rock.

The Columbia River has been blocked many times between Hood River and Beacon Rock, first by volcanic flows and more recently by massive landslides. The southward tilting along the Gorge makes the soft Eagle Creek Formation on the north wall even more slide-prone, and it is already slippery because it retains water and sits atop slick reddish saprolite.

One of the largest slides, covering five square miles, was the Cascade Landslide (or "Dam of the Gods"). About 700 years ago, much of Greenleaf Peak and Table Mountain broke off, probably triggered by an earthquake, and pushed the river against the south canyon wall, moving the main channel over a mile. The slide, which is still slowly moving, blocked the Columbia and formed a lake that extended as far east as Umatilla; this rock barrier was probably the legendary Bridge of the Gods. The river immediately began tearing away at the dam, gradually lowering the 500 foot deep lake and cutting the S-shaped course, the Great Cascades of the Columbia, that survived until the arrival of the Corps of Engineers.

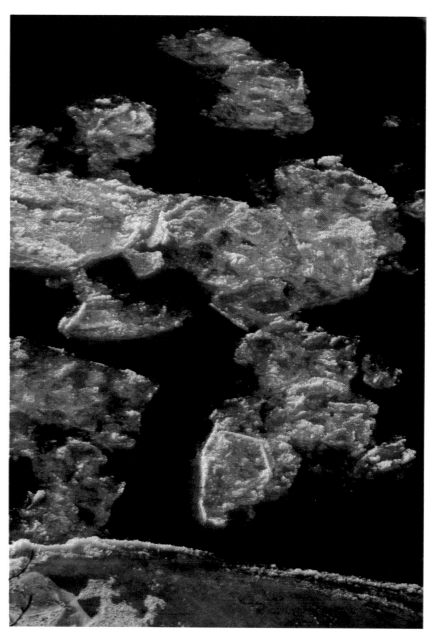

Ice flows on the Sandy River.

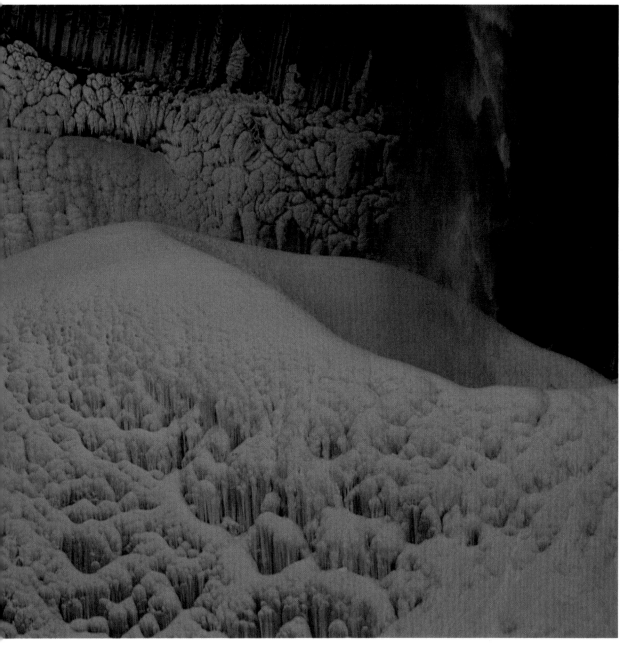

The Columbia Gorge, especially around the Cascades, is notorious for its rain and violent storms. Pioneer journals almost unanimously condemn the Gorge's foul weather; Peter Burnett, who explored the Gorge in 1843 with John Fremont's expedition, noted that, "We had been told it rained oftener and harder at the Cascades than at almost any other point in Oregon; and, to our injury, we found it true."

West of the Cascade Mountains is a marine climate: wet, with moderate temperature changes because of the ocean. East of the range is a continental climate: drier and more extreme. The seasons begin west of the Cascades about a month later than they do in the arid plateau east of the divide. The Columbia Gorge is a barometer, equalizing pressure between the two sides of the mountains, and sometimes the rain forest and the desert collide in the Gorge, brewing up the famous storms. Winds from the west are most common, but those from the plateau are more severe; 100 mile–an–hour gales are not uncommon.

A 1921 storm dropped 54 inches of snow on The Dalles, but recent years had been mild, and the river seldom froze anymore — until the Januaries of 1979 and 1980, when snowstorms immobilized the Gorge for weeks. The most beautiful storms are the Gorge's "silver thaws," its extraordinary freezing rains. They occur when icy winds from the east blow down the Gorge beneath warm rains that are moving inland from the Pacific. When the supercooled raindrops fall, they freeze; soon all the trees and bushes are coated with an inch or two of glistening ice. Then the excitement begins; branches, whole trees and powerlines come crashing down from the excess weight. One such "silver thaw" buried my van beneath about one–third of the limbs of a giant fir, and branches crashed against my cabin with explosions sounding like mortar attacks.

Latourell Falls.

When the government put a weather station on Crown Point,
the instruments were blown away by the next storm.

Climates are not all that meet in the Columbia Gorge. The quick change in rainfall—more than 75 inches annually at Cascade Locks, 30 inches in Hood River, less than 14 inches at The Dalles—makes possible an enormous variety of plant life. In addition to the west–to–east transition from lush rain forest to grassy oaklands to sagebrush desert, the north (Washington) bank is sunnier, the south (Oregon) side steeper, damper, colder and darker, thus promoting even more diversity. Many plant species reach the limit of their range in the Gorge; balsamroot and bitterroot from the Rockies are abundant around Bingen, and blue lilac and white lilac reach as far north as the Klickitat River.

More than a dozen plant species grow only around the Gorge. Rocky Mountain and subalpine plants that usually grow at high elevations are found near sea-level, isolated in the Gorge's darker side–canyons, evidently the remaining islands of plants from the Ice Ages when boreal (cold weather) plants spread throughout the Northwest. About six thousand years ago, a warm period enabled xeric plants (warm and dry tastes) to move northward, from the Rogue River toward Puget Sound. Some, such as the Oregon white oak, slipped through the Gorge, probably along the sunnier north bank, and survived at the eastern end, even after the rest of the chapparal plants retreated southward.

Swamp behind Wind Mountain.

Columbine.

Near Dog Creek Falls.

Animals also used the Gorge as a path for expanding their range: squirrels and salamanders moved east; the muskrat, a species of vole and the tiny (and endangered) Columbian white-tailed deer expanded their ranges to the western side of the Cascades. The Larch Mountain salamander lives only in the Gorge, and there is an isolated population of coral king snakes in Klickitat County.

Attracted by the salmon, bald eagles and California condors were once common along the river. Waterfowl, including Canadian geese and wood ducks, filled the lakes along the Columbia in such large numbers that Lewis and Clark complained that they couldn't sleep because of the noise. Swans were numerous, as were mountain beavers and regular beavers. Harbor seals swam as far inland as the Deschutes River, and the Washougal River was named Seal River by Lewis and Clark.

When humans first visited the Columbia Gorge, mammoths and mastodons still roamed the land. By the time the white people came, the lower Columbia had attracted an exceptionally large Native American population. Sir George Simpson, the head of Hudson's Bay Company, wrote in 1824 that: "The native population on the banks of the Columbia River is much greater than in any other part of North America that I have visited; as from the upper Lake to the coast the shores are actually lined with Indian Lodges at the Fishing Season."

Bald eagle.

47

3. Salmon and Roots

"The Dalles" from the government's 1853-5 Pacific Railroad Report.

I like to think an Indian is someone who thinks of himself as an Indian. The Indian is a person who has a strong sense of himself as an individual in terms of his environment, his relationship with it ... he has a rich oral tradition, a strongly developed artistic sense, a sense of propriety, that is, appropriateness. The movies have a difficult time in depicting, creating an image of <u>an</u> Indian, I think, mainly because of his diversity. There are over 300 Indian societies in the U.S.A., over 100 living languages.

— N. Scott Momaday

The Cascade Indians, from whom I am descended, are practically extinct. They and their relations downstream were decimated by the diseases that were the advance forces of white settlers into the lower Columbia region. Fewer than one in ten of the natives survived the epidemics of smallpox and malaria, and most of the survivors were sent to other tribes' reservations. My great-great-grandfather, Tumalth, one of the many Cascade chiefs, miraculously survived the plagues and remained in the Gorge — only to be arrested by the U.S. Army and hung, evidently unjustly. Bullets, however, were only occasionally necessary to displace natives in the Columbia Gorge.

"Chinook Travelling Lodge" by Paul Kane.

Maggie McLaughlin, or Tumsuppa, one of the last Cascade Indians, was born at the Cascades in 1889.

The rapid demise of these long-evolving cultures makes it difficult to paint an accurate picture of life in the Columbia Gorge before Europeans arrived. Many artifacts have been lost; wood perishes quickly in the wet climate, and bulldozers and reservoirs have destroyed most of what might have survived. Even so, the more durable artifacts — arrowheads, fishing net weights — were found in amazing numbers. A collector once filled a pickup truck with fishing net weights in an hour.

The natives of the Gorge left no written history; the most complete records we now have of these people are the journals of the first white explorers, especially those of Lewis and Clark. These accounts, however, often contradict each other; and when reading these descriptions of the "savages," it is helpful to remember the rationalizing that was apparently necessary for settlers who displaced native peoples.[10] Also, the first smallpox epidemic had already swept up through the Gorge over a decade before the coming of Lewis and Clark, killing half of the population; the Chinookan cultures the explorers observed were in shambles. My ancestors' better days had already passed.

The Cascade Indians were one of the numerous Chinookan-speaking tribes that lived along the Columbia River from its mouth as far upriver as the Long Narrows (The Dalles), almost two hundred miles upstream; the various tribes were closely related and had similar cultures. The Cascade Indians controlled the western end of the Gorge, including the portage trail around the Great Cascades, and as far downriver as the area of the Portland Airport. The eastern-most Chinookan peoples, who lived near the Long Narrows, were the Wish-hams, or Wish-coms. Those from the north bank are now usually referred to as Wishrams, those from the south bank Wascos. Between the Cascades and Wish-hams, and often included with one or the other of them, were the Chilluckittequaw (White Salmon) Indians north of the river and the Dog (Hood) River bands—referred to by Lewis and Clark as the Smack Shop—on the south bank.

These villages were independent; each was a discrete social and political unit with a separate name and identity, making "tribal boundaries" difficult to define. Even the name Cascade Indian is a recent "pseudo-tribal name" used to describe villages of extended families that were also collectively known as the Watlala and the Shahala. There is some reason to believe that the Cascade Indians once called themselves the Gahláxishachk (people of the rapids).11

The classic image of the Native American is one of plains nomads, dressed in feathers and leathers, following their food supply with horses pulling their mobile homes. However, thanks to the many resources provided by the Columbia River, the Chinookan peoples were able to establish large, permanent villages. Even after horses arrived in the 18th century, they were of little interest to the canoe owners who lived along the river on the edge of thick forests — except for racing. Villages periodically moved short distances to catch fish, hunt, pick berries or harvest wappato; temporary housing was built for these excursions. Occasionally longer trips were made to trade or to dig clams at the ocean. Some Gorge villages wintered on Sauvie Island or at the junction of the Willamette and Clackamas Rivers.

Unlike other Native Americans with permanent villages, the peoples of the Columbia were not agriculturalists; they lived off the bounty of the land and the river. They were famed as traders, and their great surpluses of fish and wappato and other roots provided a handsome income and much leisure time. So much, in fact, that many early white observers considered them downright decadent. According to Ruth Underhill, the author of *Indians of the Pacific Northwest:* "These were the wealthy, leisured people in the United States in Indian days."

OREGON HISTORICAL SOCIETY

"Indian Martha" Aleck from Hood River was a friend of my grandmother.

The cultures of the Columbia peoples and the newly-arrived Euro-Americans were bound to clash. Their appearances were strikingly different, and, apparently, so were their lifestyles. Even though they often worked hard, especially during the fishing season, the Chinookan people were, to use a current expression, laid back, an attitude usually described by white newcomers as laziness or "natural indolence." Though these Native Americans admired many of the white settlers' material possessions, they generally also felt that the practice of spending most of one's waking hours working was foolish. One Chinook "princess" was known to sometimes berate her white husband for being a slave to his fur trading company:

You profess to be a great chief; but I see you hard at work every day, behind the counter and at the desk, and your time is so fully employed that you have scarcely time to eat your food, or to enjoy the society of your wife for a moment . . . [pointing to a pig in the mud] See there, that is the true chief; he has no labour to perform, like a slave; when hungry, his food is served up, he fills himself, he then lies down in the soft mud, under the influence of the warming rays of the sun, sleeps and takes his comfort.

The intense effort and relentless pace of the white settlers puzzled the native peoples. John Townsend, a naturalist who visited the Gorge in the 1830s, noted that "their business is seldom of a very urgent nature"; and he seemed surprised that such "primitive" people could be happy, although at times a sympathy for "Indian time" crept into his writings:

In one of these houses we found men, women, and children, to the number of fifty-two, seated as usual, upon the ground, around numerous fires, the smoke from which filled every cranny of the building, and to us was almost stifling, although the Indians did not appear to suffer any inconvenience from it. Although living in a state of the most abject poverty, deprived of most of the absolute necessaries of life, and frequently enduring the pangs of protracted starvation, yet these poor people appear happy and contented. They are scarcely qualified to enjoy the common comforts of life, even if their indolence did not prevent the attempt to procure them . . . In a short time the chief joined us, and our party stopped for an hour, and had a "talk" with him. He told us, in answer to our questions, that his people had fish, and would give them for our goods if we would sleep one night near their camp, and smoke with them. No trade, of consequence, can ever be effected with Indians, unless the pipe be first smoked, and the matter calmly and seriously deliberated upon. An Indian chief would think his dignity seriously compromised if he were expected to do any thing in a hurry, much less so serious a matter as a salmon or beaver trade; and if we had refused his offered terms, he would probably

have allowed us to pass on, and denied himself the darling rings, bells, and paint, rather than infringe a custom so long religiously practised by his people.

John Wilbur Attwell, a son of the first white settlers at Cascade Locks, had a more objective view of American Indian life:

Many of the settlers think of the Indian as a savage. Some of us who have lived with 300 Indians as close neighbors see them much different than the cowboy who can not speak of word of Chinook sees them ride by his camp. When you talk with them in their own language and they trust you and you trust them, you get a much better picture. They do not have any prisons or jails that are full of lawbreakers as the white man does who criticizes their uncivilized ways.

They have few artificial wants, they have abundance of leisure time for conversation. They think foolish of the paleface's laborious manner of life. The paleface fences a piece of land, plows it, builds a house and barn, raises a crop, harvests it and sells it to buy food and clothes. Indians catch salmon, shoot deer, tan hides to make clothes and doesn't need to pay taxes.

James "Monty" Attwell, John's brother, also wrote, rather more idyllically, about the Gorge natives' value system and labors:

In a way these people were the richest people in North America. Not rich in gold and silver. If they had been able to dig these metals from the mountains as the White man did, the Indians would have thought of them as another ornament, like bear claws, eagle's talons or sea shells. Wealth to them was something to wear or eat.

The Columbia River abounded in fish which was their favorite food. In a few months the families could get enough food to last them all year. They smoked and dried the salmon, picked and dried berries, acorns and different roots. The balance of their time was given to art, war, ceremonies and feasting.

Smoke was always thick from the open fires with no chimneys but they did not seem to mind. Meat was hanging from the ceiling being smoked and cured. The Indian women would cook their meals around these fires and often be singing while doing it. They were always busy, cutting up the meat, tanning the hides, making baskets or bead work.

Alexander Ross, an early fur trader, at times also saw the romantic aspects of native life along the lower Columbia:

On a fine day it is amusing to see a whole camp or village, both men and women, here and there in numerous little bands, gambling, jeering and laughing at one another, while groups of children keep in constant motion, either in the water or practicing with bow and arrow, and even the aged take a lively interest in what is passing, and there appears a degree of happiness among them, which civilized men, wearied with care and anxious pursuits, perhaps seldom enjoy.

Most shocking to the Europeans was the physical appearance of the lower Columbia's inhabitants. Ethnologist Albert Gatschet called the Chinookan peoples a "populous, Mongol-featured nation," and historian Herbert Bancroft noted their most eye-catching feature—flattened foreheads:

In physique the Chinook can not be said to differ materially from the Nootka. In stature the men rarely exceed five feet six inches and the women five feet. Both sexes are thick-set, but as a rule loosely built . . . Different ages and nations strive in various ways to remodel and improve the human form. Thus the Chinese lady suppresses the feet, the European the waist, and the Chinook the head . . . The Chinook idea of facial beauty is a straight line from the end of the nose to the crown of the head.

John Townsend described in his journal how deeply-ingrained the beautification was:

A custom prevalent, and almost universal amongst these Indians, is that of flattening, or mashing in the whole front of the skull, from the superciliary ridge to the crown. The appearance produced by this unnatural operation is almost hideous, and one would suppose that the intellect would be materially affected by it. This, however, does not appear to be the case, as I have never seen, (with a single exception, the Kayouse,) a race of people who appeared more shrewd and intelligent. I had a conversation on this subject, a few days since, with a chief who speaks the English language. He said that he had exerted himself to abolish the practice in his own tribe, but although his people would listen patiently to his talk on most subjects, their ears were firmly closed when this was mentioned; "they would leave the council fire, one by one, until none but a few squaws and children were left to drink in the words of the chief." It is even considered among them a degradation to possess a round head, and one whose caput has happened to be neglected in his infancy, can never become even a subordinate chief in his tribe, and is treated with indifference and disdain, as one who is unworthy a place amongst them.

At first Townsend was shocked by the head-flattening:

I saw, to-day, a young child from whose head the board had just been removed. It was, without exception, the most frightful and disgusting looking object that I ever beheld. The whole front of the head was completely flattened, and the mass of brain being forced back, caused an enormous projection there. The poor little creature's eyes protruded to the distance of half an inch, and looked inflamed and discolored, as did all the surrounding parts. Although I felt a kind of chill creep over me from the contemplation of such dire deformity, yet there was something so

stark-staring, and absolutely queer in the physiognomy, that I could not repress a smile; and when the mother amused the little object and made it laugh, it looked so irresistibly, so terribly ludicrous, that I and those who were with me, burst into a simultaneous roar, which frightened it and made it cry, in which predicament it looked much less horrible than before.

Caw-wacham, a Cowlitz woman, died shortly after Paul Kane painted this portrait; Kane was blamed and had to flee.

However, Townsend soon became used to the Chinook look:

There are here several young children; beautiful, flat-headed, broad-faced, little individuals. One of the little dears has taken something of a fancy to me, and is now hanging over me, and staring at my book with its great goggle eyes. It is somewhat strange, perhaps, but I have become so accustomed to this universal deformity, that I now scarcely notice it.

Babies spent a few months in the cradle/press, and artist Paul Kane observed that babies cried when pressure was taken *off* the moss–padded boards and quieted when it was again applied. Nearly all of the Chinooks at the river mouth had flat heads, which evidently caused no permanent physical or mental impairment, but as one moved upstream, fewer of the men did. The last person in the Gorge with a flattened head was a woman born about 1880; she lived near Hood River until her death in 1973.

Franchère explained the relationship between flat foreheads and slavery:

However, among the barbarians, the flat head is an indispensable ornament and when we said that this fashion seemed to us to violate nature and good taste, they answered that it was only the slave who did not have a flat head.

Slaves, do, in fact, have round heads, and are never permitted to flatten those of their infants, destined to bear the chains of their fathers. The natives get their slaves from neighboring tribes and from the interior, giving beads, beaver skins, and other things in exchange. They treat them well enough as long as their services are useful; when old and unable to work, they are neglected and left to die in misery. When they die they are thrown, without ceremony, under tree trunks or at the edge of the woods.

"Round-heads" could sometimes obtain their freedom through hard work but could never become chiefs. People sometimes became slaves as a result of criminal acts or debts, but most slaves were obtained through trade with tribes to the south, primarily the Klamaths. Sometimes even slaves had slaves. Of course, having a flat head was no protection against being enslaved outside Chinookan cultures.

Although the Cascade Indians had few slaves, slavery was once a common practice among Northwest coastal tribes—just as it was in the U.S.A. back then. (Clark even brought his slave, York, along on the trip; and the expeditions' sponsor, President Thomas Jefferson, owned slaves.) Slavery among Indians also ended after the Civil War.

"A Cascade Indian," also by Paul Kane.

53

When it came to clothing, the Chinookan peoples were minimalists; they were well–enough acclimated to their environment that clothing was seldom needed—except for fashion. Elaborate costumes were not common, but jewelry and makeup were. Lt. Broughton, the first European to reach the Gorge, said their decoration "surpassed all the other tribes with paints of different colours, feathers, and other ornaments." Paint would sometimes suffice, although it was usually only applied for ceremonies. According to Lewis and Clark, the native men occasionally wore breechcloths to "conceal the parts of generation." The women usually wore skirts; Gabriel Franchère described the style:

Only in winter time do they throw around their shoulders a panther skin or some kind of cape, made from the skins of wood rats sewn together. In addition to the cape, in winter they wear a conical hat, made from fibrous roots, which give the feeling of being rainproof.

Besides the cape, women wear a kind of skirt or petticoat, made of cedar bark which they hang around their waists and which comes to the middle of the thighs. The skirt is somewhat longer in back than in front and is made in the following manner: They tear off the fine bark of cedar, soak it as one soaks hemp, and lay it out in fringes. Then, taking a cord of the same material they divide the fringes around and tie them down firmly. With such a wretched garment they manage to hide the private parts.

Children sometimes wore robes made from grey squirrel skins. Blankets woven from the long hairs of dogs and of mountain goats were obtained from coastal tribes, but these disappeared in the Gorge soon after the Hudson's Bay Company blankets were introduced. (A U.S. Navy officer recommended a shipment of *good* blankets for gifts "for an Indian would rather go naked than wear a bad one.") Sandals and moccasins were occasionally worn on long trips.

When dressed up, some Chinookan people wore bracelets and bead earrings and inserted shells through their pierced noses. The most commonly used shell was dentalium, *hiqua*, found in deep waters off Vancouver Island. Dentalium also served as a currency of sorts in prehistoric times.

The Chinookan people had high cheekbones, flat noses and, except for some elderly men, usually plucked any facial hair. Poor eyesight and teeth were common. Early journals describe marks on their bodies, but differ as to whether they were tumors or wounds self–inflicted to demonstrate bravery. Tattooing was common among the Lower Chinooks.

Lewis and Clark and many other explorers thought the Indian women along the lower Columbia were homely, but not all early visitors agreed. Captain Gray's seventeen–year–old fifth mate wrote of the Chinooks:

They are very numerous and appear very civil (not even offering to steal). The men are straight limbed, fine looking fellows and the women are very pretty. They are all in a state of nature except the females, who wear a leaf apron. But some of our gentlemen that examined them pretty close and near, both within and without, reported that it was not a leaf but a nice wove mat in resemblance.

The first white explorers wrote that Indian women along the lower Columbia were less oppressed than the women of prairie tribes, but Chinookan society was still a man's world. Women raised the children, cleaned the fish, gathered roots and berries, fetched water and wood, prepared most meals and, according to Gabriel Franchère: "Among their primary duties is the making of cane mats, baskets for the gathering of roots, and hats of very ingenious design." Men fished, hunted, cooked for guests, did much of the sewing, cut down trees, carved canoes and fought wars — and evidently still had enough time to lie around being "indolent."

Political alliances were often forged through marriages, and smart chiefs often married the daughters of other powerful chiefs. Gabriel Franchère described nuptial vows on the lower Columbia:

Marriages are conducted with a good deal of ceremony. When a young man seeks a girl in marriage, his parents make the proposals to those of the intended bride, and when it has been agreed upon what presents the future bridegroom is to offer to the parents of the bride, all parties assemble at the house of the latter, whither the neighbors are invited to witness the contract. The presents, which consist of slaves, strings of beads, copper bracelets, haiqua shells, etc., are distributed by the young man, who on his part receives as many and sometimes more, according to the means or the munificence of the parents of his betrothed. The latter is then led forward by the old matrons and presented to the young man . . . The men are not very scrupulous in their choice and take small pains to inform themselves what conduct a young girl has observed before her nuptials, and it must be owned that few marriages would take place if the youth would only espouse maidens without reproach on the score of chastity . . . Polygamy is permitted; there are some who have as many as four or five wives; and although it often happens that the husband loves one better than the rest, they never show any jealousy, but live together in the most perfect concord.

Most of the child care was left to older sisters and the elderly. Some early accounts deplored the poor treatment accorded the elderly, especially the blind, but others said they "were treated with much respect." Chief Skameniah, of the village located near Dallesport, was disturbed by the "new" Americans' rudeness and accent on youth:

Our council is made of our old men who have had much experience, but you are governed by young men with little experience. In our councils, the one to speak rises while the others observe complete silence. When he is through he sits down and we wait a few minutes to be sure that he has finished speaking. I visited your court in The Dalles and see your young counsels shouting at each other and the judge rapping his hammer and calling until he is hoarse trying to keep order until one can cite his side of the case.

Village decisions were made by consensus, and though men held the power, women played a strong and vocal role in the councils. Chiefs were basically family patriarchs and had to be wealthy enough to provide welfare payments. Land was "owned" in common by the tribe, and the various tribes knew the limits of their territories, even though strict, set boundaries did not exist. Women could also increase their influence through wealth, and Chinookan women became more powerful after the white traders arrived; the traders preferred to deal with them rather than with the more dangerous—and less amusing—men.

Trading in the Northwest was complicated by the number of languages. The dialects of the Chinookan villages were especially difficult, and few Europeans learned them. Accordingly, translators were much in demand. Paul Kane the nomadic painter, complained:

I would willingly give a specimen of the barbarous language of these people were it possible to represent by any combination of the letters of our alphabet the horrible harsh spluttering sounds which proceed from their throats, apparently unguided either by the tongue or lips. It is so difficult to acquire a mastery of their language that none have been able to attain it unless those who have been born amongst them.

They have, however, by their intercourse with the English and French traders succeeded in amalgamating, after a fashion, some words of each of these tongues with their own and formed a sort of Patois, barbarous enough certainly, but still sufficient to enable them to communicate with the traders.

This "patois," Chinook Jargon, based primarily on Nootka and Chinook words, was the common language used among Northwestern tribes, much as sign language was on the plains; English and French and other European words were incorporated to facilitate fur trading. Some words had stranger sources. For instance, *pehlten,* meaning unusual or absurd, came from the behavior of a bizarre "Judge" Pelton at Fort George.[12]

The Chinookan peoples played a central role in trading because they resided along the lower Columbia, the main trade route, and large quantities of trade goods could easily be moved on their huge canoes. Lewis and Clark admired these boats. Clark described them as "neeter made than any I have ever seen and calculated to ride the waves, and carry emence burthens." Patrick Gass of the same expedition added that, "The natives of this country ought to have the credit of making the finest canoes, perhaps in the world, both as to service and beauty; and they are no less expert in working them when made." The expedition's journals note:

The larger of the canoes was ornamented with a figure of a bear in the bow and a man in the stern, both made of painted wood and very neatly fixed to the boat. In the same canoe were two Indians finely dressed with round hats ... When they embark, one Indian sits in the stern and steers with a paddle; the others kneel in pairs in the bottom of the canoe, and, sitting on their heels, paddle over the gunwale next to them... In the management of these canoes women are equally expert with the men, for in the smaller boats, which contain four oarsmen, the helm is generally given to the female.

Franchère wrote about the boats:

Their canoes, or pirogues, are all made of cedar and are all of one piece. We have seen some that were five feet wide and thirty feet long. These are the largest, and they often carry twenty-five or thirty men. The smallest carry only two. The sharp pointed bow extends four or five feet. It thus serves to break the waves that otherwise would swamp the canoe when the water on the river is rough. Their oars, or paddles, are of ash and about five feet long; the top end has a grip very much like the top of crutch. The blade is cut in a half–moon shape, having two sharp points.

James Swan described how the impressive boats were made, an involved process that required several weeks even after European tools arrived:

The manufacture of a canoe is a work of great moment with these Indians. It is not every man among them that can make a canoe, but some are, like our white mechanics, more expert than their neighbors. A suitable tree is first selected, which in all cases is the cedar, and then cut down. This job was formerly a formidable one, as the tree was chipped around with stone chisels, after the fashion adopted by beavers, and looks as if gnawed off. At present, however, they understand the use of the axe, and many are expert choppers. When the tree is down, it is first stripped of its bark, then cut off into the desired length, and the upper part split off with little wedges, till it is reduced to about two thirds the original height of the log. The bow and stern are then chopped into a rough shape, and enough cut out of the inside to lighten it so that it can be easily turned. When all is ready, the log is turned bottom up, and the Indian goes to work to fashion it out. This he does with no instrument of measurement but his eye, and so correct is that, that when he has done his hewing no one could detect the least defect. When the outside is formed and rough–hewn, the log is again turned, and the inside cut out with the axe. This operation was formerly done by fire, but the process was slow and tedious. During the chopping the Indian frequently ascertains the thickness of the sides by placing one hand on the outside and the other on the inside. The canoe is now again turned bottom up, and the whole smoothed off with a peculiar–shaped chisel, used something after the manner of a cooper's adze. This is a very tiresome job, and takes a long time. Then the inside is finished, and the canoe now has to be stretched into shape. It is first nearly filled with water, into which hot stones are thrown, and at the same time a fire of bark is built outside. This in a short time renders the wood so supple that the center can be spread open at the top from six inches to a foot. This is kept in place by sticks or stretchers, similar to the method of a boat's thwarts. The ends of these stretchers are fastened by means of withes made from the taper ends of cedar limbs, twisted and used instead of cords. When all is finished, the water is emptied out, and then the stem and head-pieces are put on. These are carved from separate sticks, and are fastened on by means of withes and wooden pegs or

56

Chinook lodge.

tree–nails. After the inside is finished to the satisfaction of the maker, the canoe is again turned, and the charred part, occasioned by the bark fire, is rubbed with stones to make the bottom as smooth as possible, when the whole outside is painted over with a black mixture made of burned rushes and whale oil. The inside is also painted red with a mixture of red ochre and oil. The edges all round are studded with little shells, which are the valve joint of the common snail, and, when brass-headed nails can be obtained, they are used in profusion.

Cedar, now scarce, was essential to the lives of Chinookan tribes. Cedar splits easily into boards, and its resistance to moisture was invaluable. In addition to the canoes, their houses were built of cedar planks tied together with cedar fibers. Bowls and trays were carved from the wood, and baskets were woven from cedar roots. Even the elevated burial vaults were usually made of cedar planks. Using an elk–horn wedge and a stone or wood knot club (hardened by fire), workers split cedar into long planks about two inches thick and up to two feet wide; smoothing was done with abrasive stones.

The cedar lodges that lined the Columbia up to the Long Narrows were huge. Lewis and Clark described one Shahala (Cascade) lodge at the village of Nechacokee west of the Gorge as being 226 feet long and divided into seven 30 foot square apartments connected by a long hallway. The permanent homes were usually sunk into the ground one to six feet; the vertical plank walls rose a few feet above the ground. The sloping roofs were made of overlapping cedar planks or bark, and an adjustable opening near the top let light in and smoke out. The small, oval door was covered by a hanging plank or mat, and a ladder descended to the sunken living room. Lewis and Clark described the inside of one of the lodges at Cathlakaheckit, a Cascade village that was excavated before being finally destroyed in 1979 to make a spillway for a new powerhouse at Bonneville Dam:

As we passed the village of four houses, we found that the inhabitants had returned, and we stopped to visit them. The houses are similar to those already described, but larger, from thirty-five to fifty feet long, and thirty wide, being sunk in the ground about six feet, and raised the same height above. Their beds are raised about four feet and a half above the floor, and under them are stored their dried fish, while the space between the part of the bed on which they lie and the wall of the house is occupied by the nuts, roots, berries, and other provisions, which are spread on mats. The fireplace is about eight feet long, and six feet wide, sunk a foot below the floor, secured by a frame, with mats placed around for the family to sit on. In all of the houses are images of men of different shapes, placed as ornaments in the parts of the house where they are most seen.

57

The interior decoration was described in greater detail by fur trader Alexander Henry when he visited the village of Cathlayackty, which was supplanted by the town of Cascade Locks:

The front planks of the beds are carved and painted in various styles. At the end of each range are some broad upright planks, on which figures are rudely carved, somewhat resembling fluted pillars. At the foot of the chief's bed are planted in the ground at equal distances four figures of human heads, about two feet high, adorned with a kind of crown, and rudely painted. Beside these figures are erected in the ground two large, flat painted stones. On the side of each partition, facing the fireplace, are carved and painted on the planks, uncouth figures of eagles, tortoises, and other animals, some of them four feet long. The colors are white, red, black, and green; the sculpture, in some instances, is not bad.

Temporary homes were often little more than huts, wigwams made of sapling frames and covered with mats or cedar bark, but many — especially those at favorite fishing spots or wappato patches — were replicas of the permanent lodges, although they seldom had sunken floors. Some families used the same planks for all their houses, and moving meant carrying the walls and roof, board by board, between the frames of the two homes.

Permanent villages were occasionally moved a short distance. Sgt. Patrick Gass of Lewis and Clark's expedition speculated on the reason:

Passed a place where there was a village in good order when we went down; but has been lately torn down, and again erected a short distance from the old ground where it formerly stood. The reason for this removal I cannot conjecture, unless to avoid the fleas which are more numerous in this country than any insects I ever saw.

Indeed, indoor living was not up to modern standards; besides the fleas, there was the smoke from the fires and the cold drafts (due to the lack of finished lumber).[13] But it was the fleas that were the primary scourge of the villages, and the scratching victims had no way of dealing with them except to pack up the town and move it a quarter–mile or so away, surrendering the former site to the vermin. Lewis and Clark dreaded the Chinookan lodges because of the fleas. And, of course, the flea problem was aggravated by the many dogs that ran around the villages. Naturalist John Townsend grew to hate these dogs:

Attached to this establishment, are three other houses, similarly constructed, inhabited by about thirty Indians, and at least that number of dogs. These, although very useful animals in their place, are here a great nuisance. They are of

no possible service to the Indians, except to eat their provisions, and fill their houses with fleas, and a stranger approaching the lodges, is in constant danger of being throttled by a legion of fierce brutes, who are not half as hospitable as their masters.

Fur trader Alexander Ross also wrote about the hospitality — and the dogs:

On the score of cheer, we might here qualify the curiosity of our reader with a brief description of one of their entertainments called an Indian feast. The first thing that attracts the attention of a stranger on being invited to a feast in these parts is to see seven or eight bustling squaws running to and fro with pieces of greasy bark, skins of animals, and mats to furnish the banqueting lodge as receptacles for the delicate viands. At the door of which is placed on such occasions a sturdy savage with a club in his hand to keep the dogs at bay while the preparations are going on.

The banqueting hall is always of a size suitable to the occasion, large and roomy. A fire occupies the centre round which, in circular order, are laid the eatables, and the guests form a close ring round the whole. Every one approaches with a grave and solemn step. The party being all assembled, the reader may picture to himself our friend seated like a epicure among the nobles of the place, with his bark platter between his legs, filled top heavy with the most delicious melange of bear's grease, dog's flesh, wappatoes, olellies, amutes, and a profusion of other viands, roots and berries. Round the festive board, placed on terra firma , all the nabobs of the place are squatted down in a circle, each helping himself out of his platter with his fingers, observing every now and then to sleek down the hair by way of wiping the hands. Only one knife is used, and that is handed round from one to another in quick motion. Behind the banqueting circle sit in anxious expectation groups of the canine tribe, yawning, howling and growling; these can only be kept in the rear by a stout cudgel, which each of the guests keeps by him for the purpose of self defense; yet it not infrequently happens that some of the more daring curs get out of patience, break through the front rank and carry off his booty; but when a mishap of this kind is committed, the unfortunate offender is generally well belabored in his retreat, for the cudgels come down upon him with a well merited vengeance.

The poor dog, however, has his revenge in turn, for the squabble and howl that ensued disturbs all the dormant fleas of the domicile in motion; his troop of black assailants jump about in all directions. So that a guest by helping himself to the good things before him, keeping the dogs at bay behind him, and defending himself from the black quadrons that surround him pays perhaps dearer for his entertainment at the Columbia Cascades than a foreign ambassador does in a London Hotel!

Salmon and wappato roots were the culinary staples, the "meat and potatoes." Wappato, or arrowhead *(Sagittaria latifolia')*, once grew in abundance on the Columbia's swampy floodplain, especially near the mouth of the Willamette River; the small tuber provided vitamins and starch for the natives' diet, and was an important trade item. Wappato was dug along the lake and river banks with pointed sticks, but plants growing underwater were much harder to harvest. Lewis and Clark found a hundred small wappato canoes, "10 to 14 feet long," at one village and described how they were used by the Cascade women:

She takes one of these canoes into a pond where the water is as high as the breast, and by means of her toes, separates from the root this bulb, which on being freed from the mud rises immediately to the surface of the water, and is thrown into the canoe. In this manner these patient females remain in the water for several hours even in the depth of winter.

The other main vegetable was camas *(Camassia quamash)*, which was slightly smaller. Artist Paul Kane described camas as "a bulbous root much resembling the onion in outward appearance, but is more like the potato when cooked and is very good eating." Care had to be taken since a poisonous plant, death camas, looks similar when not in bloom.

Wappato was made into large cakes and dried for winter; fresh it was steamed, roasted or boiled. Steaming was considered the tastiest preparation. This was done by digging a hole and lining it with hot rocks; a layer of grasses was placed on the rocks, then the wappato and more grass. Finally, water was added and the hole was sealed. The slow–cooker was left for hours, preferably overnight.

The traditional method used to boil roots and fish (sometimes together as a stew) was described by Franchère:

Kitchen utensils consist of hewn–ash trays and square cedar kettles. With only these the Indians succeed in cooking their fish and meat in less time than we take with our pots and saucepans. This is the way they do it: First, they heat a number of stones red hot; then one by one, they drop these into the kettle that will hold the food. As soon as the water boils they put the fish or meat into it, and cover it with small rush mats to hold the steam. Left thus, the food is soon properly cooked.

Baskets, often beautifully decorated, were also used for boiling food. Lewis and Clark were impressed by the craftsmanship, writing that the basket "is formed of cedar bark and bear grass, so closely interwoven that it is water tight, without the aid of either gum or resin." Utensils were carved from wood or animal horn, often with animal designs; spoons were made by steaming and carving sheep horns.

"Wishham Basket Maker" by Edward Curtis. "Sally bags" —tall, flexible baskets used to carry items —were unique to the Narrows area.

Artist Paul Kane described how the Indians started fires before matches arrived:

The fire is obtained by means of a small flat piece of dry cedar, in which a small hollow is cut, with a channel for the ignited charcoal to run over; this piece the Indian sits on to hold it steady, while he rapidly twirls a round stick of the same wood between the palms of his hands, with the point pressed into the hollow of the flat piece. In a very short time sparks begin to fall through the channel upon finely frayed cedar bark placed underneath, which they soon ignite. There is a great deal of knack in doing this, but those who are used to it will light a fire in a very short time.

A small bow with a string wrapped around the shaft of the fire stick was also sometimes used.

The plentiful berries in the Gorge — including blackberries, huckleberries (blueberries) famous for their sweetness, raspberries, strawberries and salmonberries—added to the bounty. (Salmonberries were also used ceremonially; one would be placed in the mouth of a live salmon that was then released to insure the health of the species.) Roots of other plants such as lupine, fern, thistle, cattail and skunk cabbage were also occasionally eaten, as were mushrooms, black lichen and hazel nuts.

Native tobacco (*Nicotiana quadrivalvis*) was the only domestic plant cultivated by the Columbia peoples (although most of it was obtained in trade with tribes to the south); it was "never sowed by the Indians near the villages lest it should be pulled and used before it comes into perfect maturity." Stumps were burned and the ashes used to make the plants grow larger. The inner bark of the red willow was also smoked, and wild crab apple bark was sometimes chewed.

The favorite fish were salmon (especially Chinook salmon) and steelhead, the large ocean-going trout. Salmon were often split (always lengthwise; cross-cut steaks were frowned upon for religious reasons) and propped open with sticks beside a fire, a method still favored by most Northwest salmon connisseurs. Depending upon which end of the Gorge one fished at, salmon to be stored was either dried over fires or in the sun. It was then usually ground into a powder; a pinch of this dried fish was enough to flavor a winter bowl of soup. Fish and other food were ground with a stone pestle on a stone mortar or wood tray, and berries were sometimes added to the fish.

The number of fish caught during the annual salmon runs often depended on how much help a fisherman had, such as how many wives to clean the fish. A chief told Paul Kane that he "had taken as many as 1,700 salmon, averaging 30 pounds each, in one day." Salmon were usually speared or dip–netted at the falls, but seines (large nets) were most common elsewhere. Platforms were built out over good fishing spots, as they still are on the Klickitat and Deschutes Rivers. Most fishing spears were forked, with barbs on each side; iron hooks replaced bone in later times. Many giant sturgeon were caught with hooks attached to long, strong cords made of Indian hemp.

Tumalth, my great–great–grandfather, also used to catch smelt, a tiny anchovy–like fish once known as candlefish because they burn when dried. They were caught with nets or "fish rakes" (ingenious curved devices that, when turned upside down over the canoes, released the fish). Smelt were strung on cords and smoked over the fires.

Hunting was secondary to fishing, but mammals taken included deer, elk, bear and mountain goats; bows and arrows or snares were usually used. Nets were occasionally strung across lakes during foggy or windy weather to snare ducks or geese. Monty Attwell wrote that he once almost shot a swimming duck before he realized that it was a decoy on the head of an Indian sneaking up on a flock of ducks. Sometimes game birds were pulled underwater and drowned so their struggles would not be heard by nearby birds. Townsend witnessed a unique method of catching swans:

The ducks and geese, which have swarmed throughout the country during the latter part of the autumn, are leaving us, and the swans are arriving in great numbers. These are here, as in all other places, very shy; it is difficult to approach them without cover; but the Indians have adopted a mode of killing them which is very successful; that of drifting upon the flocks at night, in a canoe, in the bow of which a large fire of pitch pine has been kindled. The swans are dazzled, and apparently stupefied by the bright light, and fall easy victims to the craft of the sportsman.

This drawing and the one on page 55 are from James Swan's The Northwest Coast, *1857.*

Even after guns were introduced (in the days before repeating firearms), many natives continued to prefer bows; gunpowder proved dangerous, the noise scared the game, and many arrows could be fired in the time it took to reload a rifle. As to accuracy, Lt. Broughton's aid, Thomas Manby, wrote that "they seldom miss a mark at twenty yards, and will often kill a bird at forty." The local bows were short, so that they could be easily carried through the thick woods. Lewis and Clark described them:

The bow is extremely neat, and being very thin and flat, possesses great elasticity. It is made of the heart of the white cedar, about two and a half feet in length; two inches wide at the center, whence it tapers to the width of half an inch at the extremeties; and the back is covered with the sinews of elk, fastened on by means of a glue made from the sturgeon. The string is formed of the same sinews. The arrow generally consists of two parts; the first is about twenty inches long, and formed of white pine, with a feather at one end. At the other end is a circular hole, which receives the second part, formed of some harder wood, and about five inches long, and secured to its place by means of sinews. The barb is either stone, or else of iron or copper.

Arrows were often made from split cedar, sometimes in two pieces so that the shaft could be retrieved and used again with a new arrowhead; they were rounded and straightened with heated and oiled grooved stones. Ancient quarries for Wascoite arrowheads have been found on the banks above the Long Narrows. Trader Alexander Henry found a surprise in a quiver captured at the Great Cascades:

I had the curiosity to examine the quiver of arrows belonging to the prisoner. It was made of a black bear cub [hide], and held 70 loose arrows, with a parcel of 10 more arrows carefully tied up with cedar bark. These last were examined minutely, and found to be poisoned. Small strips of rattlesnake skin were stuck to the barbs by means of some glutinous substance, which Casino told us was also poison. The arrows were painted green, red, brown, and yellow. Some of the barbs are so loosely fixed in their sockets as to be left in the flesh they penetrate when the shaft is pulled out.

Arrows were also dipped in rattlesnake venom. A man in Ross Cox's party was hit by one of these special arrows during a skirmish at the Cascades but was saved by one of his trading party's Indian employees:

One of the Iroquois hunters sucked the blood from his wound . . . this saved the poor fellow's life, as we had reason to think the arrow was poisoned. The day after, the arm became quite black from the wrist to the shoulder.

Before the Euro-Americans arrived, food was so abundant that there was no need to fight over it; war, accordingly, was a ritualized affair. Trader Alexander Ross called the Chinookan peoples "a commercial rather than a warlike people." War game futurists should appreciate this account by Gabriel Franchère of a savage battle:

Since all the villages form so many little sovereignties, differences often arise among them, whether among chiefs or among the people. These disputes usually are resolved by payments equivalent to the injuries. However, when the offense is grave, as in the case of murder (which is pretty rare), or the stealing of a woman (and this is common enough), the injured parties, assured of the help of a number of young men, prepare for war.

In this case, an unusual ritual for the savage world is adhered to. Before initiating any warlike action, they warn the enemy of the day on which they will attack their village. In this procedure they do not follow the custom of nearly all the other American Indians, who seize upon their enemies without warning and kill or capture men, women, and children. To the contrary, these people embark in canoes, which on such occasions are paddled by women, approach the enemy village, enter into parly, and do all they can to settle their differences amicably. Sometimes a third party, observing a strict neutrality as mediator, attempts to negotiate an agreement between the two warring tribes. If those who demand justice do not obtain it to their liking, they retire a little distance, paint their faces, and combat begins and continues for some time, with fury on both sides. But as soon as one or two men are killed, the army that has lost them acknowledges itself defeated and the battle stops. If it is the party of the village attacked who are the losers, the attackers do not leave until they have received some payment.

Ross Cox added:

Should the day be far advanced, the combat is deferred, by mutual consent, till the next morning, and they pass the intervening night in frightful yells, and making use of abusive and insulting language to each other. They generally fight from their canoes, which they take care to incline to one side, presenting the higher flank to the enemy; and in this position, with their bodies quite bent, the battle commences. Owing to the cover of their canoes, and their impenetrable armour, it is seldom bloody.

Their warlike weapons are the bow and arrow, with a curious kind of double-edged sword or club, two and a half feet in length by six inches in breadth. They seldom, however, fight near enough to make use of this formidable instrument. It is not necessary to mention that in their warlike expeditions their faces and bodies are painted in various colours, and with the most grotesque figures.

Psychological terror seemed to be the favorite weapon. The war dances that preceded the actual confrontations were "an awkward kind of dance, accompanied by yellings and gestures not of an entertaining description." British physician John Scouler described a war dance held near Fort George in 1825:

About 50 men paraded from the vicinity of the fort to the beach, they moved at a most grotesque pace, keeping their feet in the same position with respect to another as nearly as possible. On their progress to the beach they fired their fowling pieces & set up the most disagreeable howling I ever heard; they then formed a circle & continued their dance, making a general yell every two or three minutes. Each of them [wore] a war dress consisting of dressed elk skin, which went over them like a shirt without sleeves. The warriors were painted of every sort of colour, but principally black, red & yellow. Their music consisted of a number of shells of Pecten marina tied to a stick, which they rattled during the whole of their manoeuvres.

The "war dress," half-inch thick elkskin armor called a *clamon*, became a major trade item. They were arrow–proof, but not bullet–proof at close range; some white traders intimidated possibly–hostile natives by folding a clamon double and firing a bullet through it. Another type of armor was made of thin sticks tied together with beargrass.

Gambling and sports were evidently much more exciting than warfare to the natives of the lower Columbia. Monty Attwell remembered the exuberant gambling at a village across from Cascade Locks:

The Indians loved to gamble and play games. They did not need to worry over paying taxes, the value of stocks and bonds, or how the elected officials were doing in Washington, D.C. The men were big gamblers at heart. When visiting Indians came from the coast or east of the mountains and camped nearby, it wouldn't be long until Chall chall or similar games were in progress. I have often watched but never joined into the games of chance. When I was a boy of 12, Chief Trujons (often called True Johns) asked Celly, my older half brother, to take him across the river in a rowboat. Celly invited me along. We landed on the north bank just above the chutes and walked down around Bradford's Landing to the small lake later known as Icehouse Lake. Here on the meadow alongside the lake were hundreds of Indians camped. This lake is at the north end of the man–made Bridge of the Gods, and before the railroad and highway came through there was a nice meadow alongside of the lake.

Great games of gambling were in progress so I might tell a little about one of these games. Several groups were in separate places with much noise going on. The players sit opposite each other, usually three on a side; sometimes they sit cross–legged and other times they kneel facing each other, three on a side. Each side has a number of small sticks stuck in the ground for keeping score and the players have two small polished bones like beaver teeth. When all is ready and the stakes or prizes are put up, a song is struck up with the pounding of sticks on a piece of wood, sort of keeping time; this not only makes more excitement but also adds to the confusion. One side starts passing the small bones from one fist to another with great speed, nimbly crossing and recrossing arms. The players muffle their wrists, fists and fingers with bits of fur or leather in order the better to elude and deceive their opponents. The quickness of the motions and the muffling of the fists make it almost impossible for his opponents to guess which hand holds the bones, which is the main point of the game. While the player is doing all this maneuvering, his opponent eagerly watches his motions, trying to discover which fist contains the bone. He points with lightning speed at the fist he thinks the bone is in, the player at the same time extends his arm and opens the fist; if it is empty the player draws his arm back and continues, while the guesser must forfeit one of his ten score sticks. If the guesser hits upon the fist that contains the bone, the player must give the guesser one of his ten sticks and cease playing while the opponent tries his hand at juggling the bone from fist to fist. When one side wins all ten sticks of his opponent, the game is over.

Artist Paul Kane noted that Chinooks play "with much equanimity, and I never saw any ill-feeling evinced by the loser against his successful opponent." He described many of the games:

Another game which I have seen amongst them is called Al–kolloch, and is one that is universal along the Columbia river. It is considered the most interesting and important as it requires great skill. A smooth level piece of ground is chosen, and a slight barrier of a couple of sticks laid lengthwise is made at each end; these are 47 or 50 feet apart and a few inches high, the two opponents, stripped naked, are armed each with a very slight spear about 3 feet long and finely pointed with bone; one of them takes a ring made of bone or some heavy wood, and wound around with cord about three inches in diameter, on the inner circumference of which are fastened six beads of different colours at equal distances, to each of which a separate numerical value is attached; the ring is then rolled along the ground to one of the barriers and is followed at the distance of 2 or 3 yards by the players, and as the ring strikes the barrier and is falling on its side the spears are thrown so that the ring may fall on them; if only one of the spears should be covered by the ring the owner of it counts according to the coloured bead over it. But it generally happens, from the dexterity of the players, that the ring covers both spears, and each count according to the colours of the beads above his weapon. They then play towards the other barrier, and so on until one party has attained the number agreed upon for game.

They also take great delight in a game with a ball, which is played by them in the same manner as by the Cree, Chippewa and Sioux Indians. Two poles are erected about a mile apart, and the company is divided into two bands armed with sticks, having a small ring or hoop at the end with which the ball is picked up and thrown to a great distance, each party then strives to get the ball past their own goal. There are sometimes hundreds on a side, and the play is kept up with great noise and excitement. At this game they also bet heavily, as it is generally played between tribes or villages.

William Perry wrote in *The Columbian* about an eyewitness account of one such lacrosse game played near Fort Vancouver:

One American journalist who was here before the Hudson's Bay Company settled at Vancouver, saw a team from Wappato [Sauvie] island play a team from up–river. To be exact, the teams were composed of all the able bodied men from both villages. According to the writer, the natives discarded the last vestige of clothing and played entirely naked. Incidentally, they had wagered their canoes, their blankets, their slaves and their squaws on the outcome of the game. This inspired the women to cut long switches with which they belabored their spouses from the rear, urging them on to greater effort.

Women played a game called *omintook*, using dice made from beaver teeth, but I can't find any evidence of them wagering husbands.

Kane wrote that the "Chinooks are fond of racing, at which they bet considerably; they are expert jockeys and ride fearlessly." My great–grandfather, Johnny Stooquin, Kalliah's Wishram second husband, was a jockey. The main hazards at the Indian racetrack near the Great Cascades (by North Bonneville) were low branches over the track, and one family story tells of Stooquin not ducking low enough and getting knocked off his horse. Kalliah ran over yelling, *"memaloose Johnny, memaloose Johnny!* [Johnny's dead]"; fortunately, he survived.

Monty Attwell wrote about the Indian Heaven race track and the method used to break the wild horses:

Indians from east of the mountains would join the local Indians at the huckleberry fields south of Mt. Adams. Many different tribes would camp near each other at these fields. Horse races and gambling were at their best. One tribe would bring their best horse to race another tribe's best horse. The races were much like the white man's races at an early fair. One chief would enter his best horse and another chief would bring his greatest horse. Bets were wagered and at a signal, the two fast horses were off.

There were always a few young bucks along the sidelines with their own horses, and after the champions passed, they would take off after them but were soon left far behind. Between the races the famous wild huckleberry was picked. Cedar trees were stripped of their bark for making baskets to bring the berries home in aboard the horses.

The Cascade Indians did not have many horses like the Indians east of the mountains, but they had a few. I have often watched them break a horse to ride. They rode bareback and did not have saddles until the white man brought them. It is near impossible to stick aboard a wild horse without a bridle and saddle so they overcame this by blindfolding the horse until the young buck was aboard, then a couple of bucks would tie his feet together under the horse's belly and the horse was unblindfolded and turned loose. The wild horse could not throw the rider and as long as it didn't go completely over backward the young buck survived and the horse wore itself down. The young buck might be bleeding from his nose and ears but he had won the match.

Large gatherings usually centered around catching salmon or collecting berries or roots; these were times of great festivities. They were ideal for meeting other tribes and were the source of many marriages. "First products ceremonies" were common to celebrate the annual coming of salmon, roots and berries; other important ceremonies included puberty rites for women.

Historian Bancroft wrote that at festivals the Chinookan people were "fantastically dressed and gaudily decked with paint, they are wont to jump about on certain occasions in a hopping, jolting kind of dance, accompanied by songs, beating of sticks, clapping of hands, and occasional yells, the women usually dancing in a separate set." Dr. W.F. Tolmie, of the Hudson's Bay Company, rode out with Dr. McLoughlin in 1833 to inspect the farms upriver from Fort Vancouver; he described how the native dances had been altered by Christianity:

There were several large fields of wheat & pease & one of barley —with rich and extensive natural meadows. Heard a loud howling & approaching a party of from 30 to 40 Indians, men, Women & children performing their devotions. They formed a circle two deep & went round & round, moving their hands as is done in skulling, exerting themselves violently & simultaneously repeating a monotonous chaunt loudly. Two men were within the circle & kept moving rapidly from side to side making the same motion of arms, & were I am told the directors or managers of the ceremony.

Having continued this exercise for several minutes after we beheld them becoming more & more vehement & excited, they suddenly dropped on their knees & uttered a short prayer & having rested a short time resumed the circular motion.

During the ceremony so intent were they that not one eye was once turned toward us, although we stood within a few yards.

The worship of "pagan idols," however, was still common among Chinookan peoples. Europeans were appalled by the Indian's "superstitions"; in turn, natives had trouble believing many Biblical tales, such as the ones about Jonah being swallowed by a whale and a snake giving an evil apple to Adam and Eve. Townsend wrote about the Indians' objects of worship:

In almost every house, there is a large figure, or idol, rudely carved and painted upon a board, and occupying a conspicuous place. To this figure many of the Indians ascribe supernatural powers. Chief Chinamus says that if he is in any kind of danger, and particularly, if he is under the influence of an evil spell, he has only to place himself against the image, and the difficulty, of whatever kind, vanishes at once. This certainly savors of idolatry, although I believe they never address the uncouth figure as a deity. Like all other Indians, they acknowledge a great and invisible spirit, who governs and controls, and to whom all adoration is due.

The Indians frequently bring us salmon, and we observe that, invariably, before they part with them, they are careful to remove the hearts. This superstition, is religiously adhered to by all the Chinook tribe. Before the fish is split and prepared for eating, a small hole is made in the breast, the heart taken out, roasted, and eaten in silence, and with great gravity. This practice is continued only during the first month in which the salmon make their appearance, and is intended as a kind of propitiation to the particular deity or spirit who presides over the finny tribes.

Lewis and Clark wrote about another ritual involving salmon; the first fish caught was cut up and fed to the children, a gesture thought to speed up the coming of the salmon runs. And it was mandatory that the first fish be eaten before sunset on the day it was caught.

The Chinooks' religion was intimate with nature; they believed in spirits and conversed with the spirits of plants, trees, rivers, mountains and animals since they, too, had souls. Each person had a personal guardian spirit that was obtained in a spirit quest. A youth would journey to a "power spot" and fast until a guardian spirit was revealed in visions. Symbols of the individual's guardian spirit, the so-called "idols," were then carved on cedar planks to protect the person's home —and his or her grave after death. Illness was often caused by an evil spirit entering one's body.[14]

The Chinookan peoples had two types of doctors: *keelalles,* who administered medicines; and *etaminuas,* who healed the soul. One Indian doctor, who lived near Underwood, was Co-la-ta-chen, "Lone Wolf," who "was considered aloof and lonely." Even though many native medicinal plants have been found to be effective, Dr. Townsend, the physician/naturalist, was no more impressed with native medicines for the body than he was with local cures for the soul:

Wounds are treated with an application of green leaves, and bound with strips of pine bark, and in some febrile cases, a sweat is administered. This is effected by digging a hole two or three feet deep in the ground, and placing within it some hemlock or spruce boughs moistened with water; hot stones are then thrown in, and a frame work of twigs is erected over the opening, and covered closely with blankets to prevent the escape of the steam. Under this contrivance, the patient is placed; and after remaining fifteen or twenty minutes, he is removed, and plunged into cold water.

Their mode of "making medicine," to use their own term, is, however, very different from this. The sick man is laid upon a bed of mats and blankets, elevated from the ground, and surrounded by a raised frame work of hewn boards. Upon this frame two "medicine men" (sorcerers) place themselves, and commence chaunting, in a low voice, a kind of long drawn, sighing song. Each holds a stout stick, of about four feet long, in his hand, with which he beats upon the frame work, and keeps accurate time with the music. After a few minutes, the song begins to increase in loudness and quickness.

These medicine men are, of course, all imposters, their object being simply the acquisition of property; and in case of the recovery of the patient, they make the most exorbitant demands of his relations; but when the sick man dies, they are often compelled to fly, in order to escape the vengeance of the survivors, who generally attribute the fatal termination to the evil influence of the practitioner.

The Cascade Indians "buried" their dead in elevated vaults, usually on islands (probably to protect the corpses from large animals). Mourning mothers cut off their hair and sang death chants, and there was a strict prohibition against speaking the names of the dead.

A bural site near the Cascades, one of the few on the mainland, was described by Major Osborne Cross in 1849:

A burial ground was high on the banks of the Columbia river in sight of the rapids and one of the most secluded and romantic spots nature could have formed. It was in a large, dense grove of hemlock and fir trees whose limbs spread a shade over the whole spot, almost excluded the light of heaven which seemed, in defiance of the foliage, to shed its rays now and then upon the tombs of the dead.

Lewis and Clark also wrote about the graveyard and noted that it was

This interior of a Chinook lodge was painted by Paul Kane.

customary to leave personal possessions with the deceased, probably for use in the afterlife:

About half a mile below this house, in a very thick part of the woods, is an ancient burial place: it consists of eight vaults made of pine or cedar boards closely connected, about eight feet square and six in height; the top secured, covered with wide boards sloping a little, so as to convey off the rain; the direction of all of them is east and west, the door being on the eastern side, and partially stopped with wide boards decorated with rude pictures of men and other animals. We found in some of them four dead bodies, carefully wrapped in skins, tied with cords of grass and bark, lying on a mat in a direction east and west: the other vaults contained only bones, which were in some of them piled to the height of four feet: on the tops of the vaults, and on poles attached to them, hung brass kettles and frying-pans with holes in their bottoms, baskets, bowls, sea-shells, skins, pieces of cloth, hair, bags of trinkets and small bones, the offerings of friendship or affection.

This site has since been obliterated by a highway and a railroad; the vaults at another Cascade burial site on nearby Sullivan Island were burned by early white settlers because of the stench. The tribe's other main graveyard, the one where Tumalth was laid to rest (temporarily), was Bradford Island, now the site of the Bonneville Dam Visitor Center. Most villages near The Dalles used Memaloose Island (by Lyle); another large island further upstream was used primarily by the Yakimas.

Although "no Indian would ever take a thing from a bural site," the sacred dead–houses were the best sources of artifacts and were frequently robbed by white people. "Relic hunters" even carried off the flat skulls and bodies. One group of early settlers on a steamboat were met with a "volley of bullets" when they tried to visit my ancestors' burial vaults on Bradford Island; they retreated.

John Townsend was more persistent in his quest to steal the corpse of a child with a flattened head to ship back east "for science," but even his nosing around the burial grounds was not appreciated:

I have been very anxious to procure the skulls of some of these Indians, and should have been willing, so far as I alone was concerned, to encounter some risk to effect my object, but I have refrained on account of the difficulty in which the ship and crew would be involved, if the sacrilege should be discovered; a prejudice might thus be excited against our little colony which would not soon be overcome, and might prove a serious injury. As we turned to leave the place, we found that we had been narrowly watched by about twenty Indians, whom we had not seen when

we landed from our boat. After we embarked, we observed an old withered crone with a long stick or wand in her hand, who approached, and walked over the ground which we had defiled with our sacrilegious tread, waving her enchanted rod over the mouldering bones, as if to purify the atmosphere around, and exorcise the evil spirits which we had called up.

Near Fort William downstream, where the Chinooks put the dead in canoes high in trees, temptation finally got the best of Townsend:

Upon examination, what was my surprise to find a perfect, embalmed body of a young female, in a state of preservation equal to any which I had seen from the catacombs of Thebes. I determined to obtain possession of it, but as this was not the proper time to carry it away, I returned to the fort.

That night, at the witching hour of twelve, I furnished myself with a rope, and launched a small canoe, which I paddled up against the current to a point opposite the mummy tree. Here I ran my canoe ashore, and removing my shoes and stockings, proceeded to the tree, which was about a hundred yards from the river. I ascended, and making the rope fast around the body, lowered it gently to the ground; then arranging the fabric which had been displaced, as neatly as darkness allowed, I descended, and taking the body upon my shoulders, bore it to my canoe, and pushed off into the stream. On arriving at the fort, I deposited my prize in the store house, and sewed around it a large Indian mat, to give it the appearance of a bale of guns. Being on a visit to the fort, with Indians whom I had engaged to paddle my canoe, I thought it unsafe to take the mummy on board when I returned to Vancouver the next day, but left directions with Mr. Walker to stow it away under the hatches of a little schooner.

On the arrival of this vessel, several days after, I received, instead of the body, a note from Mr. Walker, stating that an Indian had called at the fort, and demanded the corpse. He was the brother of the deceased, and had been in the habit of visiting the tomb of his sister every year. He had now come for that purpose, from his residence near the "tum-water"[15] [cascades], and his keen eye had detected the intrusion of a stranger on the spot hallowed to him by many successive pilgrimges. The canoe of his sister was tenantless, and he knew the spoiler to have been a white man, by the tracks upon the beach, which did not incline inward like those of an Indian.

The case was so clearly made out, that Mr. W. could not deny the fact of the body being in the house, and it was accordingly delivered to him, with a present of several blankets, to prevent the circumstance from operating upon his mind to the prejudice of the white people. The poor Indian took the body of his sister upon his shoulders, and as he walked away, grief got the better of his stoicism, and the sound of his weeping was heard long after he had entered the forest.

Edward Curtis took this 1910 photo of Kalliah's sister, Virginia Miller, near the mouth of the Wind River.

Most of Memaloose Island, the famous burial site near Lyle, has been covered by the backwaters of Bonneville Dam. The Indian "death-houses" were removed, but a single gravestone is still visible. It marks the grave of the only white person ever buried on the island, Victor Trevitt; he came to The Dalles in 1854 and became a well-known politician. Trevitt, who died in 1883, asked to be buried on Memaloose Island, reasoning: "In the resurrection, I'll take my chances with my friends, the Indians."[16]

4. *The Long Narrows*

"The Commencement of the Dalls" in 1849.

At the Dalles the vast river is jammed together into a long narrow slot of unknown depth cut sheer down in the basalt. This slot or trough is about a mile and a half long and about sixty yards wide at the narrowest place. At ordinary times the river seems to be set on edge and runs swiftly but without much noisy surging with a descent of about twenty feet to the mile. But when the snow is melting on the mountains the river rises here sixty feet, or even more during extraordinary freshets, and spreads out over a great breadth of massive rocks through which have been cut several other gorges running parallel with the one usually occupied. All these inferior gorges now come into use, and the huge, roaring torrent, still rising and spreading at length, overwhelms the high jagged rock walls between them, making a tremendous display of chafing, surging, shattered currents, counter–currents, and hollow whirls that no words can be made to describe. A few miles below the Dalles the storm–tossed river gets itself together again, looks like water, becomes silent and with stately, tranquil deliberation goes on its way, out of the gray region of sage and sand into the Oregon woods.

—JOHN MUIR

Tsagiglalal, "She Who Keeps On Watching," still overlooks the site of the Long Narrows. The basket and sally bag were made by Wascos; the bowl was made from mountain sheep horn. Art Wolfe photo.

The late Long Narrows, where the Columbia River once turned on its side, was the best fishing spot of all, even better than Celilo Falls and the Short Narrows just upstream and the Great Cascades downstream, where my people lived. Celilo is now the best known of the fishing sites, but only because it was the last to be covered by a reservoir and was altered in historic times to improve fishing. Countless salmon filled the eddies around these constrictions, gathering their strength before attacking the next set of rapids. Salmon were so thick that a spear thrown blindly would usually hit a twenty–pound fish. During the annual runs, a native fisherman could net or spear more than a ton of salmon a day. These fishing sites were also exceptional because they were low on the Columbia, and further upstream the bodies of exhausted salmon, nearing death, had lost valuable oil.

Considering what a rich fishing hole it was, it is not surprising that the Long Narrows — also known as the Grand Dalles and Five Mile Rapids — may be this nation's longest continuously occupied village site. At the Wishram village, near what is now called Horsethief Lake, Lewis and Clark noted "a mound of about 30 feet above the Common leavel, which mound has some remains of houses and has every appearance of being artificial." Artificial it was, layer upon ancient layer of garbage. This was the famous Wakemap Mound; an excavation revealed two thousand years of history. Other ancient sites were found nearby, and petroglyphs and rock art were plentiful on the surrounding cliffs along the north bank, where the best building sites and fishing spots were. Wakemap Mound and most of the petroglyphs have now been buried by the backwaters of The Dalles Dam.

Across the river at Five Mile Locks was a similar mound, named the Road Cut Site because highway, railroad and canal engineers got there before the archaeologists. Dr. L. S. Cressman excavated this stratified mound and, using carbon–14 dating, found that the site had been continuously occupied for more than 10,000 years! Native Americans probably had lived near the Long Narrows even earlier, but the most recent deluge would have removed earlier artifacts — along with their makers.

As in the legends, the first human residents of the Gorge had a rough time. The salmon were not cooperating, and nearly every waking hour had to be spent searching for food: a sparse hunter–gatherer economy. Clubs and rocks were used to kill small game. Bolas, long cords with grooved rocks attached to the ends, were developed; when thrown,

bolas tangled birds and felled them. At the Atlatl Valley site near Wakemap, many worked pieces of stone were found; they are probably the weights for atlatls, "throwing–sticks," which enabled hunters to hurl spears and darts faster and farther.

The first points and knives were made from bone and antler, but stone, including chert, petrified wood and even basalt, was usually used after the natives learned to shape and sharpen rocks by chipping. Scrapers were made by sharpening one edge of a thin stone, and knives and points became thinner and sharper — "mule ears" — as skills improved. Bows were a later addition to their arsenal, and many arrow smoothers have been found.

Stone pestles were common for grinding nuts, sunflower seeds, roots, choke–cherries and other foods. Trees were felled and wood split with bone, antler and wood wedges hammered by polished stone mauls; then the wood was worked with stone chisels that were lashed to wood handles. Awls were usually made from deer or elk bones.

Many of the animals that these people hunted were becoming scarce; a long hot period, an altithermal beginning about 7500 years ago, gradually dried up many of the lakes that once covered much of the Great Basin east of the mountains. Living along the Columbia River became increasingly attractive, especially as fishing methods improved. Dip nets were developed, and nets were strung across the river. The grooved rocks used to hold down these nets were once common along the Columbia's banks. "Leads," willow and stone fences, were sometimes used to steer salmon into shallow water. Fresh water mussels were also eaten.

The gradual change to the present temperate climate greatly increased the food supply. The cultures slowly developed; as living became easier with the improving fishery, leisure time resulted in beautiful stone art. Head scratchers (made of bone), horn spoons, and stone bowls and mortars were among the practical items ornately decorated.

Much prehistoric art was evidently created purely for aesthetic purposes. Detailed effigies, good–luck charms, were carved from stone, bone and antler (although possibly only in recent times). Stone and bone beads of all sizes have been found along the Columbia by the tens of thousands; the hole was usually drilled first, using a stone–tipped shaft spun between the palms. Many objects were painted, and "paint-pots" used to mix paints are common around village sites; the most common paint was a red ochre mixed with animal or fish oil.

Celilo Falls by Frank Knapp, who took many priceless photos of the Gorge.

Petroglyphs that were once near the Long Narrows.

Before "Lake" Celilo buried it, the area around the Long Narrows was famed for its petroglyphs and pictographs. (Petroglyphs are chipped into the cliff face; pictographs are painted on.) The local style incorporated an "exposed skeleton motif," the stylized depiction of vertebrae and ribs on the outside of people and animals. The mountain sheep (once common in the region) was the most popular animal subject, possibly because it was so difficult to hunt. Unique to the Columbia Gorge is the "Spedis Owl," a wonderful abstract owl designed with huge concentric eyes.[17]

Early homes in the Gorge were probably simple brush or mat shelters. As the population grew, these abodes were replaced by round, earth-covered homes sunken into the ground; a hole in the center of the roof allowed people to enter and smoke to escape. The frames and cedar plank supports for the dirt roof eventually evolved into the huge board houses that Lewis and Clark found at the ancient village site of Wakemap. Circular, semi-subterranean lodges with dirt roofs, about sixteen feet across, were still in use at what is now Bingen and above the Long Narrows when the first white people came.

Trade goods from long distances arrived at the Long Narrows because of its key location on the travel corridor between the increasingly different cultures separated by the mountain range. Trade goods found near Wakemap Mound included pipestone from Minnesota, turquoise from the Southwest, dentalium from Vancouver Island and copper that must have come from Alaska, Canada or the Great Lakes.

By the time Lewis and Clark "discovered" the Columbia Gorge, its native residents had developed a rich civilization; the Long Narrows had become the region's major trade mart. Trails radiated out from the Narrows and from Celilo Falls, and thousands of Indians from the surrounding countryside gathered every year to fish, visit, meet friends and lovers, trade, sing, compete in games, gamble and party. This entire stretch of river became an annual summer-long county fair, a crowded campground of temporary mat shelters.

Lewis and Clark described the "cash crop" at the Long Narrows and at Celilo:

Here is the great fishing-place of the Columbia. In the spring of the year, when the water is high, the salmon ascend the river in incredible numbers. As they pass through this narrow strait, the Indians, standing on the rocks, or on the ends of wooden stages projecting from the banks, scoop them up with small nets distended on hoops and attached to long handles, and cast them on the shore.

They are then cured and packed in a peculiar manner, first exposed to the sun on scaffolds erected on the river banks. When sufficiently dry, they are pounded fine between two stones, pressed into the smallest compass, and packed in baskets or bales of grass matting about two feet long and one in diameter, lined with the cured skin of a salmon. The top is likewise covered with fish skins, secured by cord passing through holes made in the edge of the basket.

Packages are then made, each containing twelve of these bales, seven at bottom, five at top, pressed close to each other, with the corded side upward, wrapped in mats and corded.

The expedition saw 10,000 pounds of salmon stacked up at the Wishram village — and this was the fall after all but the permanent residents had already left, taking their salmon with them.

The use of prime fishing spots was inherited, but others were allowed to share the site and the catch. At Celilo the roar of the falls drowned out conversation and led to a unique custom. Fishermen netted the salmon, killed them with clubs and threw them into nearby piles. Other Indians were allowed to take fish, but if the fisherman was having bad luck and needed all of his fish, he slapped his buttocks twice, meaning

don't take any. According to Alexander Ross, however, fishing was not the only lure for the summer tourists; they were "all foreigners from different tribes throughout the country, who resort hither not for the purpose of catching salmon, but chiefly for gambling and speculation, not in fish, but in other articles."

From downriver, the coast and Puget Sound came dried clams and mussels, whale and cedar products, shells (especially precious dentalia), beads, canoes, baskets and, after the whites arrived, such trade goods as the beloved Hudson's Bay Company blankets. From the south came baskets, obsidian, wocas (water-lily seeds), Indian tobacco and slaves. From the plateau to the east came animal robes (including buffalo), meat, kouse and other plants, pipestone, feathers and, after 1730, horses and plains-style garments. Ideas were also exchanged; the Long Narrows-Celilo Falls area became a major communications center where diverse cultures made alliances and shared stories, religions, politics and history in peace. The permanent inhabitants of the Narrows were the Wish-hams, the easternmost Chinookan peoples. "Scattered premiscuisly" at the head of the Long Narrows, Lewis and Clark found a bustling village of 21 huge houses — "the first Wooden houses since we left those in the vicinity of the Illinois" — inhabited by a few hundred year-round residents. This village was *Nixluidix*, the famous Wishram of Washington Irving's *Astoria*. Across the river, near the oldest mound, were the longhouses of the Wishrams' powerful cousins, the Wascos.

Paul Kane painted these salmon-drying racks at the Narrows.

Edward Curtis took this 1910 photo of the Yakima wife of Mnainak, the influential son of the chief of the Skin village at Celilo Falls.

Upstream from the Narrows, the river banks and the surrounding plateau were inhabited by another people, Sahaptin-speaking tribes.[18] A few of these people lived along the Columbia year-round, but most had two homes and spent the winters along tributaries, where they found firewood, game and shelter from the sand and harsh winds of the Gorge. Sahaptin settlements upriver from the Long Narrows included the Skin and Wyam villages at Celilo Falls and four large towns on Miller Island (at the mouth of the Deschutes River). The Tenino, Tygh and John Day tribes, sometimes referred to as the Warm Springs bands, spoke the Tenino dialect of the Sahaptin language and moved between the banks of the Columbia and the wooded headwaters of tributaries flowing from the south. The tribes bought cedar from downstream and floated logs down the Deschutes to supply firewood and house frames for villages at the barren eastern end of the Gorge; their descendants still fish from platforms on the Deschutes River.

The Yakimas, a large Sahaptin-speaking tribe, wintered far up the Yakima River, but in the summer moved down to the Columbia to fish and trade. Their relations, the Klickitats, occupied the prairies north of the Gorge and shared villages with Chinookan people around the mouth of the White Salmon River. Like the Cascades, the Klickitats used their strategic position between coast and plateau cultures to become great traders; they were the middlemen between the Narrows/Celilo trade mart and Puget Sound villages. Major Sahaptin-speaking tribes that inhabited the vast plateau east of the Gorge included the Umatilla and the Walla Walla.

The Sahaptin people also depended on the salmon but were more mobile on land than were my Chinookan ancestors, especially after horses arrived in the early 1700s. By early spring, Sahaptin food supplies usually dwindled, so small groups began hunting and digging early roots; expeditions visited seasonal camps to harvest camas, bitterroot and kouse. In summer, large camps were set up at fishing sites for the salmon runs. After the last runs, these people moved to the mountains, where the men hunted, and the women picked berries; meat and berries were dried, and hides were tanned for the winter. Winters were spent in large camps, where tools and clothing were made or repaired. Snowshoes made travel possible, but winter was a quiet season characterized by storytelling and religious ceremonies (the most important being Guardian Spirit dancing).[19]

The nomadic lives of most Sahaptins required homes that could be easily transported. Mats, usually made from tule or cattail rushes, were relatively light and flexible; pole tripods were used as frames. Small, round mat houses were used at the river and at other food-gathering spots, but in the winter, large mat longhouses, as much as 100 feet in length, were constructed. Like Chinook cedar longhouses, these lodges had fireplaces down the center and housed several related families.

The Sahaptin-speaking tribes did not flatten their heads, but many pierced their noses. Buckskin clothing was common — their winters were cold. Slaves were not practical in this mobile society. Chiefs were usually chosen for their achievements and the respect they commanded rather than for heredity; sometimes different individuals served various functions, such as leading hunting parties and waging warfare. Shamans, the religious leaders (and healers), also had great power. As with the Chinooks, discipline was usually maintained by shaming and strong social ostracism of criminals or rule-breakers.

Horses preceded white settlement into the Northwest by a century and radically changed the lives of the plateau people. Except for simple dugout canoes used on waterways, walking had previously been the only means of transportation. Then Spanish horses came up the trade

"The Fisherman — Wishham," also by Edward Curtis.

Umatilla mat longhouse.

routes from the Southwest, and the plateau tribes learned breeding and became famous for their Appaloosas. Horses allowed these people to carry more possessions and to roam over a much larger area for food, but greater mobility had its drawbacks: conflicts arose more often with other increasingly-mobile tribes. The horse also brought the Sahaptin people other products of the developing plains culture, such as the skin tipi and plains-style warfare. The most important change connected with the horse, of course, was the coming of the white people.

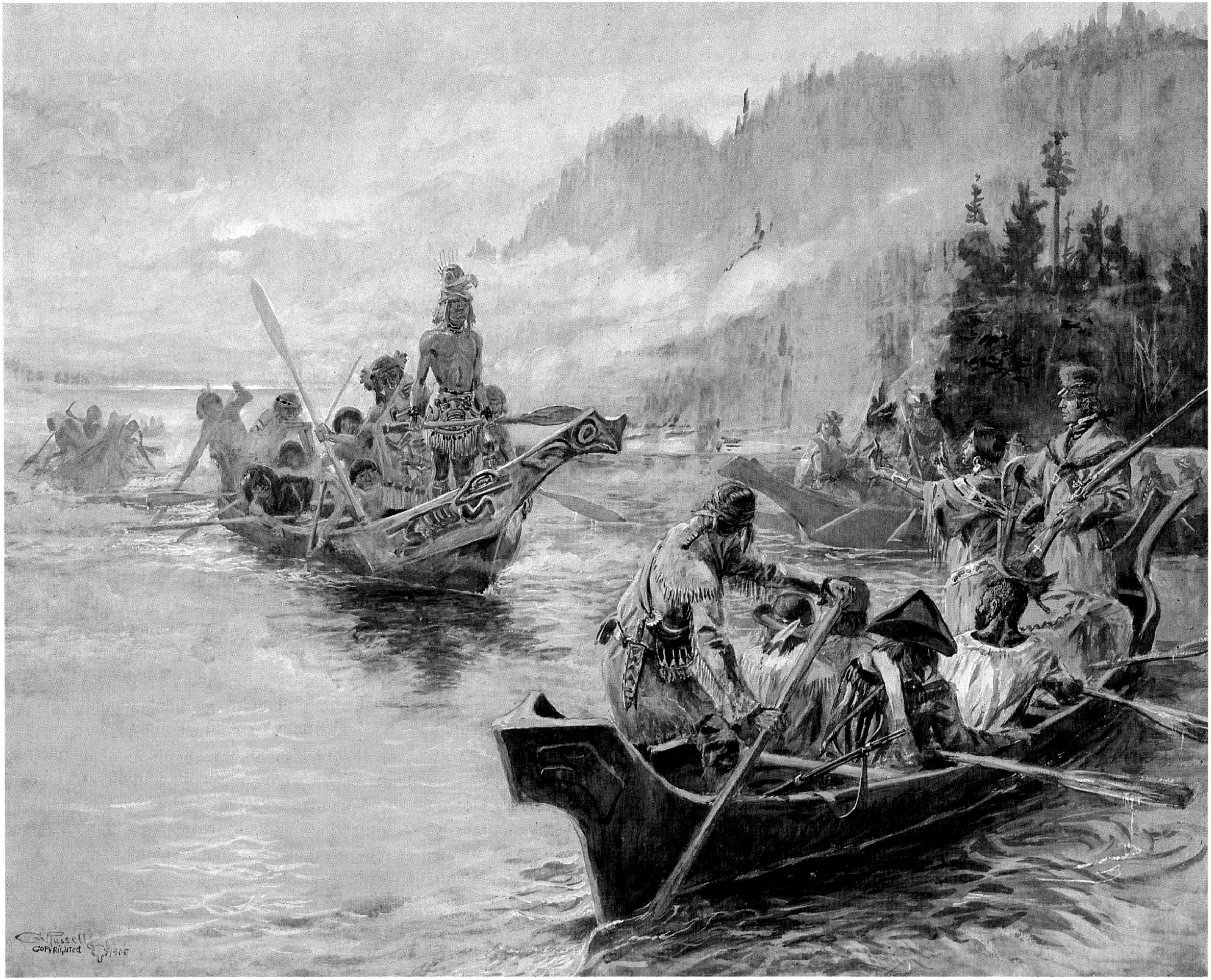

AMON CARTER MUSEUM OF ART, FORT WORTH, TEXAS

5. Illegal Aliens in Beaver Hats

That so large a river as the Columbia, making a telling current so far from shore, should remain undiscovered while one exploring expedition after another sailed past seems remarkable, even after due allowance is made for the cloudy weather that prevails hereabouts and the broad fence of breakers drawn across the bar. During the last few centuries, when the maps of the world were in great part blank, the search for new worlds was a fashionable business, and when such large game was no longer to be found, islands lying unclaimed in the great oceans, inhabited by useful and profitable people to be converted or enslaved, became attractive objects; also new ways to India, seas, straits, El Dorados, fountains of youth, and rivers that flowed over golden sands. These early explorers and adventurers were mostly brave, enterprising, and after their fashion, pious men. In their clumsy sailing vessels they dared to go where no chart or light-house showed the way, where the set of the currents, the location of sunken outlaying rocks and shoals were all unknown, facing fate and weather, undaunted however dark the signs, heaving the lead and thrashing the men to their duty and trusting to Providence. When a new shore was found on which they could land, they said their prayers with superb audacity, fought the natives if they cared to fight, erected crosses, and took possession in the names of sovereigns, establishing claims, such as they were, to everything in sight and beyond, to be quarreled for and battled for, and passed from hand to hand in treaties and settlements made during the intermissions of war.

—JOHN MUIR

Lewis and Clark came through the Columbia Gorge in 1805, and their party is usually considered the first of the "illegal aliens" to have done so.20 Juan de Fuca supposedly entered Puget Sound in 1592, but for the next two centuries few ships sailed farther north than California —unless blown there by storms.

Charles M. Russell's version of Lewis and Clark meeting my ancestors.

Fort Vancouver in 1845 by Henry Warre.

There are accounts that a Spaniard, one "Konapee," survived a shipwreck at the mouth of the Columbia River about 1725. He was a metalsmith, a skill then rare in the Northwest, and was welcomed by natives upriver. Lewis and Clark and fur traders Captain Gray, David Thompson and Gabriel Franchère all met Soto, the red-haired chief of a Gorge village. Franchère wrote:

Here we found an old, blind man who gave us a cordial reception. Our guide said that he was a white man and that he was called Soto. We learned from the old man himself that he was the son of a Spaniard who had been wrecked at the mouth of the river; that some of the crew on this occasion got safely to land, but they had all been massacred by the Clatsops with the exception of four who were spared and who married native women. Disgusted with the savage life, the four Spaniards, of whom the father of this man was one, had attempted, overland, to reach a settlement of white men, but had never been heard of again. When his father and companions left the country, Soto was quite young.

Similar stories have come down through my family. Wacomac, a Cascade Indian, told my father that my great-great-grandfather, Chief Tumalth, was about six-feet, four-inches tall, with bright red hair that hung below his waist. There are other reports of red-haired Indians along the lower Columbia in "prehistoric" times, also explained as being the progeny of a shipwrecked metalsmith, although in some versions the survivor is Scottish.

Concerned about the vigorous exploration of the Northwest by Russia and Spain, England dispatched Captain James Cook to claim a share of the spoils. Cook was killed in 1778 on his third trip, but his expedition continued on to the Orient. The Chinese, to the amazement of the crew, eagerly paid more than $100 a piece for sea otter skins that had been obtained from Northwest natives in exchange for such trifles as knives, old clothes and buttons which "did not cost the purchaser six pence sterling." One nail was worth two salmon, two nails could buy a beaver pelt, and a small sheet of copper brought four sea otter skins. Word of this profit margin spread, and fur trading vessels rushed to the Northwest. Almost one hundred U.S. ships alone had plied the coast before Lewis and Clark's visit, and Northwest furs were an important source of funds for the new nation.

Rumors of a great river in the Northwest led to continual speculation and search for the "Inland Passage" that was thought to connect the Atlantic and Pacific Oceans. Spanish Captain Bruno Heceta drew a map of "the River of the West if it exists" in 1775, but—with the previously noted exception — none of the explorers actually found the river's mouth until 1792, when Captain Robert Gray entered its mouth in the Boston Ship *Columbia Rediviva.* Later that year, English Lt. William Broughton of Captain George Vancouver's expedition ventured more than 100 miles up the Columbia, as far as the entrance of the Gorge, and renamed Wy-east for a British Admiral, Lord Samuel Hood, before turning back. Broughton thought the lower Columbia was "the most beautiful country that can be imagined." These first white explorers and traders were received warmly by the Chinooks, as described by John Hoskins, one of Captain Gray's officers:

I was received at my landing by an old chief who conducted me with Mr. Smith [another officer] to his house; seated us by a good fire; offered us to eat and drink of the best the house afforded; which was dried fish of various sorts, roasted clams and mussels. Water was our drink, handed in a wooden box with a large sea clam shell to drink out of; the chief's son attended me, opened my clams, roasted my fish, and did various other kinds of offices in which he was pleased to engage. After this entertainment we were greeted with two songs, in which was frequently repeated the words, "Wakush Tiyee a winna" or "Welcome traveling chief."

The later Lewis and Clark expedition and the Chinookan peoples generally did not get along well. The expedition considered them thievish, although this was a culture that practiced potlatch, the gaining of status through giving away one's possessions. Clark conceded that,

judging by the way these Indians consistently left their valuables unguarded for long periods, the villagers didn't steal from each other, but he wrote that the expedition "had conclusive evidence that the property of the white men is not deemed equally sacred."

It is hard to understand why the traders and explorers apparently received such mixed reactions from the Chinookan villages. The state of the villager's food supplies was no doubt a factor, and the natives probably couldn't understand why people so obviously rich weren't more generous. The predispositions and attitudes of the newcomers were probably the key factors; we see what we want to see. Captain Charles Bishop, of the British ship *Ruby,* wrote that the Chinooks always reciprocated gifts and "delighted in feeding us well and were disappointed if we did not eat heartily. They fed our dogs, too." John Townsend was also impressed by the Chinooks' generosity:

The chief welcomed me to his house in a style which would do no discredit to a more civilized person. His two wives were ordered to make a bed for me, which they did by piling up about a dozen of their soft mats, and placing my blankets upon them, and a better bed I should never wish for. I was regaled, before I retired, with sturgeon, salmon, wappatoos, cranberries, and every thing else that the mansion afforded, and was requested to ask for any thing I wanted, and it should be furnished me. Whatever may be said derogatory to these people, I can testify that inhospitality is not among the number of their failings. I never went into the house

Sea otter.

of an Indian in my life, in any part of the country, without being most cordially received and welcomed.

Such pleasant encounters were soon to end.

The cultures that Lewis and Clark met in the Gorge had already been radically changed by the booming fur trade downstream and were in the process of being decimated. With the possible exception of the survivors of early shipwrecks (who left no records, only children), no white people saw the Native Americans of the lower Columbia during their prime. European goods had preceded Lewis and Clark into the Columbia Gorge; the explorers found guns, sailors' coats, kettles and other exotic items already in use among the natives. The Cascade Indians had exchanged dried fish, mountain goat skins and wappato to their relations downstream for such goods.

European technology, such as guns and kettles, made life easier—but such trade proved to be fatal. A smallpox epidemic was also imported, probably from a visiting ship; it swept through the tribes of the lower Columbia. By 1800, it had killed about *half* the population. Most of its victims had never even seen the white newcomers who were inadvertently responsible for this new terror; the disease had come up the river, the main trade artery, along with the goods. Other undesirable imports included tuberculosis and venereal diseases.

The ethics of some of the white fur traders and the "riffraff" they brought with them had also affected the Chinookan peoples. According to trader Ross Cox:

Success was looked upon as the great criterion of a trader's cleverness; and provided he obtained for his outfit of merchandise what was considered a good return for furs, the partners never stopped to inquire about the means by which they were acquired.

The Chinooks, experienced traders long before the white fur traders arrived on the scene, usually held their own when barter was involved. Fur trader Alexander Ross noted:

The Chinook are crafty and intriguing, and have probably learned the arts of cheating, flattery and dissimulation in the course of their traffic with the coasting traders. They were up to all the shifts of bargaining. The more we gave them the more they expected and therefore the more trouble they gave us.

Many of the white traders resorted to, as one admitted, "violations of the principles of humanity." One such violation was the popular practice of kidnapping natives and either ransoming them for furs or trading

them to other tribes as slaves. Small wonder the white traders were not always warmly welcomed. The natives occasionally exacted revenge by enslaving survivors of wrecked trading ships. When the *Saint Nicholas* wrecked on the Olympic Peninsula, some Chinooks bought a Russian and an Aleut from the local tribe.

By the early years of the 19th century, sea otters were nearly extinct around the mouth of the Columbia; the local Indians turned to trading salmon—which the newcomers salted and exported—and beaver pelts obtained from inland. Because of the rapid extirpation of fur–bearing animals, white traders continuously had to seek out new areas to exploit. As competition for ever–diminishing resources increased, the natives raised the prices and became more selective, even about the size of beads. The white traders found it difficult to keep large enough stocks of conventional trading goods, so they turned to giving the Indians liquor, especially watered–down rum. A Chinook chief named Elwahco complained that his village's "children are learning to drink, gamble, to cheat and lie. Soon they will be like the Astoria white traders." Another powerful chief's son was subjected to the worst kind of scorn after a visit to Fort George:

When a son of Chief Concomly came one day to the establishment, one of our gentlemen amused himself by giving the young man some wine, and he was soon drunk. He became ill and remained in a stupor for two days. The old chief came to reproach us, saying that we had degraded his son and exposed him to the ridicule of his slaves. He begged us not to give him strong drink in the future.

Natives of the Northwest smoked ceremoniously in prehistoric times, but evidently smoking as an everyday habit came with the Europeans. Although some villages along the Columbia scorned the traders' tobacco, at least one village was so addicted by the time Lewis and Clark came down the river that its residents would accept only tobacco in trade for food. The explorers' journal describes the ritual:

The Chinooks and others inhabiting the coast and country in this neighborhood, are excessively fond of smoking tobacco, in the act of smoking they appear to swallow it as they draw it from the pipe, and for many draughts together you will not perceive the smoke which they take from the pipe; in the same manner also they inhale it in their lungs until they become surcharged with this vapour when they puff it out to a great distance through their nostrils and mouth; I have no doubt the smoke of the tobacco in this manner becomes much more intoxicating and that they do possess themselves of all it's virtues in their fullest extent; they frequently give us sounding proofs of it's creating a dismorallity of order in the abdomen.

Mayer State Park near Rowena.

Lewis and Clark, unlike most early Euro-American visitors, did not come to the Northwest for personal monetary gain; President Thomas Jefferson convinced Congress to sponsor the expedition, which carefully documented the flora, fauna and native peoples of the West. Their journal described in detail a wilderness landscape that no longer exists, except in tiny "islands," and records the first encounters many tribes had with non-Indians.

After a difficult trip across the country, Meriwether Lewis and William Clark and their party finally reached the Columbia River late in the fall of 1805. They were happy to trade their horses in for canoes and float for a change. As they approached the eastern end of the Columbia Gorge, clouds appeared just as Clark shot a crane from the sky. The local Indians, never having seen white people, hid in fright until the appearance of Sacajawea, the Shoshone wife of one of the expedition's translators. The tribe explained to her that they thought the pale explorers had come out of the clouds "and were not men."

After this dramatic entrance, Lewis and Clark portaged around Celilo Falls, but decided that their canoes were too heavy to carry around the Short Narrows. To the amazement of the Indians, themselves expert canoeists, the expedition ran the "agitated gut swelling, boiling and whorling in every direction"; the men who couldn't swim portaged such valuables as gunpowder. The expedition was edgy because its Nez Perce guides had warned the explorers that the Chinookan villagers downstream were planning to kill the invaders, but the Wishram village received them "very kindly...Peter Crusat played on the violin and the men danced which delighted the natives, who Shew every civility towards us. We smoke with these people until late at night, when everyone retired to rest." Lewis and Clark continued down to the mouth of the Columbia, where they spent a miserably wet winter in their hastily constructed Fort Clatsop. They had hoped that a trading ship would arrive to take them back to the U.S., but none came.

The expedition's trip upstream through the Gorge early the following spring was not as pleasant as the trip downstream had been. Many villages were short of food, and the first salmon weren't due for another month. Trading became difficult, frustrating. One incident may help explain the derisive term "Indian giver," a label I have always found ironic, considering who usually broke the treaties. Clark wrote:

We purchased a canoe from an Indian to day for six fathoms of wampom; he seemed satisfyed with his bargain and departed in another canoe but shortly after returned and canseled the bargain; took his canoe and returned the beeds. This is frequently the case in their method of traiding and is deemed fair by them.

Above the mouth of the Multnomah (Willamette) River, Clark stopped at a wintering village of the "Ne-er-che-ki-oo tribe of the Shah-ha-la [Cascade] Nation" and resorted to a little "magic" to obtain food:

I entered one of the rooms of this house and offered several articles to the nativs in exchange for wappato. They were sulkey and they positively refused to sell any. I had a small pece of port fire match [fuse] in my pocket, off of which I cut a pece one inch in length & put it into the fire and took out my pocket compas and set myself down on a mat on one side of the fire, and [also showed] a magnet which was in the top of my ink stand. The port fire cought and burned vehemently, which changed the colour of the fire; with the magnit I turned the needle of the compas about very briskly; which astonished and alarmed these nativs and they laid several parsles of wappato at my feet, & begged of me to take out the bad fire; to this I consented; at this moment the match being exhausted was of course extinguished and I put up the magnet etc. This measure alarmed them so much that the womin and children took shelter in their beads and behind the men, all this time a very old blind man was speaking with great vehemunce, appearently imploring his god. I lit my pipe and gave them smoke, & gave the womin the full amount [value] of the roots which they had put at my feet. They appeared somewhat passified and I left them and proceeded on.

At the large Cascade/Shah-ha-la village of Wah-clel-lah near Beacon Rock, the expedition found the native band dividing into two groups: one was heading downstream to fish at the "Falls of the Multnomah" (by what is now Oregon City), the other was moving upstream to fish at the foot of the "Great Shute" or the "Suck" (as Lewis and Clark called the Great Cascades). The expedition had considerable trouble with these "War-clel-lars," and Lewis declared them "the greates thieves and scoundrels we have met with"; they had, among other indescretions, stolen his beloved Newfoundland dog. Scammon was recovered, and the chief of the Clah-clel-lah, the next Shah-ha-la village, apologized and explained that the troublemakers were just a couple of bad apples. Lewis hoped "that the friendly interposition of this chief may prevent our being compelled to use some violence with these people; our men seem well disposed to kill a few of them. We keep ourselves perefectly on our guard."

At the next Shah-ha-la village upstream, Y-eh-hun (near Stevenson), the expedition bought more dogs to eat, a common event on the trip. The Indians didn't usually eat their dogs, but Lewis confessed:

The dog now constitutes a considerable part of our subsistence and with most of the party has become a favorite food; certain I am that it is a healthy strong diet, and from habit it has become by no means disagreeable to me, I prefer it to lean venison or Elk, and it is very far superior to the horse in any state.

At the villages along the slack water between the Great Cascades and the Narrows, Lewis and Clark saw the first horses on their return trip. For several days, the men tried unsuccessfully to buy horses, despite continual promises; and they "could secure no provisions from those people except four white Salmon trout." Finally, at a village near the Narrows, Clark noted in his diary:

I dressed the sores of the principal Chief gave some small things to his children and promised the chief some Medicine for to cure his sores. his wife who I found to be a sulky Bitch and was somewhat efficted with pains in her back. this I thought a good oppertunity to get her on my side giveing her something for her back. I rubed a little camphere on her temples and back, and applyed worm flannel to her back which she thought had nearly restored her to her former feelings. this I thought a favourable time to trade with the chief who had more horses than all the nation besides. I accordingly made him an offer which he excepted and sold me two horses.

Two more days of fruitless bargaining infuriated Clark, even though an old man served him platters of roots, pounded fish and sunflower seeds. Clark lamented:

I found it useless to make any further attempts to trade horses with those unfriendly people who only crowded about me to view and make their remarks and smoke, the latter I did not indulge them with the day. My offer was a blue robe, a callico shirt, a Silk handkerchief, 5 parcels of paint, a knife, a wampom moon, 8 yards of ribbon, several pieces of Brass, a Mockerson awl and 6 braces of yellow beeds; and to that amount I also offered my large blue blanket, my coat sword & plume, none of which seamed to entice those people to sell their horses. Notwithstanding every exertion not a single horse could be precured of those people in the course of the day.

These villagers refused to offer Lewis and Clark anything for their canoes, assuming that the boats would be abandoned anyway. But the expedition angrily chopped them up, enjoyed a last big bonfire—and then headed east.

Though trade was booming along the coast, half of the decade passed before the next group of white people visited the Columbia Gorge. British fur trading companies controlled the inland wilderness, amassing fortunes because beaver hats were fashionable; but the first white settlements on the lower Columbia were established by "new Americans." In 1810, the Winship Brothers of Boston tried to establish a "fur colony" about 40 miles up the Columbia from the coast, but they were driven out by floods and by the local Indians whose roles as traders the post threatened. The following year, however, a trading post—Fort Astoria—was built near the mouth of the Columbia by John Jacob Astor's Pacific Fur Company. Astor, a rich and powerful New York fur magnate, already controlled much of the fur trade further east; but his grandiose schemes for the Northwest were doomed to failure.

John Jacob Astor.

The Astorians sent to build the new post arrived—just barely—on the ship *Tonquin*. Its crazed captain led the crew into one disaster after another; eight men were killed when the ship tried to enter the Columbia during rough weather. After landing men and supplies at the site of what was to become Fort Astoria, the *Tonquin* sailed up the coast to trade; it was soon blown up during a battle with hostile natives.

Astor's overland party to the Columbia, led by Wilson Price Hunt and elephantine Donald McKenzie, also had a rough trip, especially when trying to get through Hells Canyon. They finally straggled down to Fort Astoria, months late. Two of the overland party, John Day and Ramsay Crooks, had been left behind upriver because they were sick. The pair were saved by Snake and Umatilla Indians, but they had a setback at the mouth of what was to later be named the John Day River. According to Crooks, who told the Astorian party that found them:

After being left by Mr. Hunt, we remained for some time with the Snakes, who were very kind to us. When they had anything to eat we ate also; but they soon departed, and being themselves without provisions, of course they left us without any. We had to provide for ourselves the best way we could. As soon, therefore, as the Indians went off, we collected some brushwood and coarse hay and made a sort of wigwam, to shelter us from the cold. We then collected some firewood; but before we got things in order, John Day grew so weak that when he sat down he could not rise again without help. Following the example of the Indians I dug some roots for our sustenance, but not knowing how to cook them, we were nearly poisoned. In this plight we fortunately let the fire go out, and for a day and night we both lay in a torid state, unable to strike fire, or to collect dry fuel. We had now been a day without food, or even a drink of water, and death appeared inevitable. But Providence is ever kind. Two straggling Indians, happening to come our way, relieved us. They made us a fire, got us some water, and gave us something to eat, but seeing some of the roots that we had collected to eat, they gave us to understand that they were poison. If we had had a fire, those very roots would have been our first food. These poor Indians stayed with us for two days and on departing they gave us about two pounds of venison.

On the same day, after the Indians had left us, a very large wolf came prowling about our hut, when John Day, with great exertion and good luck, shot the ferocious animal dead, and to his fortunate hit I think we owed our lives. The flesh of the wolf we cut up and dried and laid it by for some future emergency, and in the meantime feasted upon the skin; nor did we throw away the bones, but pounded them between stones, and with some roots made a kind of broth, which to our present circumstances we found very good. After we recovered our strength a little

and were able to walk, we betook ourselves to the mountains in search of game; and when unsuccessful in the chase we had recourse to dried wolf. For two months we wandered about, barely sustaining life with our utmost exertions. All this time we kept traveling until we happened, by mere chance, to fall on to the Umatallow River; and then following it we made the Columbia on the fifteenth of April. Our clothes being torn and worn out, we suffered severly from the cold; but on reaching this place, the Indians were very kind to us. After resting ourselves for two days with the good old man and his people, we set off, following the current in the delusive hope of being able to reach Astoria.

We had proceeded on our journey nine days without interruption and were not far from the Falls when a considerable number of Indians collected around us in the usual friendly manner. After some little time, however, one of them got up on the pretense of measuring the length of my rifle with his bow, took it in his hands; another Indian did the same with John Day's gun. The moment the two guns were in their possession the two Indians darted out of the crowd to some distance, and assuming a menacing attitude, pointed them at us; in the same instant all the others fled from us and joined the two who had taken the guns. All began to intimate to us by signs, in the most uproarious and wild manner, that some of their people had been killed by the whites.

The Indians then closed in upon us, with guns pointed and bows drawn, on all sides, and by force stripped us of our clothes, ammunition, knives, and everything else, leaving us as naked as the day we were born, and by their gestures it appeared evident that there was a disposition on their part to kill us; but, after a long and angry debate, in which three old men seemed to befriend us, they made signs for us to be off. We took off expecting every moment to receive a ball or arrow. After traveling some distance we looked back and saw the savages quarreling about the division of the booty; this gave us time to get into the hills. All that day we traveled without tasting food and at night concealed ourselves among the rocks, without fire, food or clothing. We headed back up river and in seven days we were back with our good friend Yeckatatpam who received us again and gave us these skins to cover our nakedness, as you now see.

The good old man then killed a horse, which his people cut and dried for us, and with that supply we resolved to set out this very day and retrace our steps back again to St. Louis, and when you came in sight we were in the act of tying up our meat, regretting, most of all, that we had no way of recompensing our good and faithful friend Yeckatatpam.

The elderly Umatilla was rewarded with a full set of clothes. The ordeal was too much for John Day; he became violently insane and died before he could return back east to the U.S.

Having heard of Astor's plans, the Canadian Northwest Company, known as "Nor-Westers," sent its ace geographer and explorer, David Thompson, to follow the Columbia to the Pacific, where in 1811 he surprised the newly–arrived Astorians. "Nor'Wester" Thompson soon returned upriver in the company of "two strangers" and a group of Astorians who were setting out to build an inland fort/post. Thompson explained how the couple came to join the party:

A fine morning; to my surprise, very early, apparently a young man, well dressed in leather, carrying a Bow and Quiver of Arrows, with his Wife, a young woman in good clothing, came to my tent door and requested me to give them protection, somewhat at a loss what answer to give, on looking at them, in the Man I recognized the Woman who three years ago was the wife of Boisverd, a Canadian and my servant; her conduct then was so loose that I had then requested him to send her away to her friends, but the Kootanaes were also displeased with her; she left them, and found her way from Tribe to Tribe to the Sea. She became a prophetess, declared her sex changed, that she was now a Man, dressed and armed herself as such, and also took a young woman to Wife, of whom she pretended to be very jealous; when with the Chinooks, as a prophetess, she predicted diseases to them, which made some of them threaten her life, and she found it necessary for her safety to endeavor to return to her own country at the head of this River.

Alexander Ross, a member of the party, later commented:

In the account of our voyage I have been silent as to the two strangers who cast up at Astoria, and accompanied us from thence; but have noticed already that instead of being man and wife, as they at first gave us to understand, they were in fact both women —and bold, adventurous Amazons they were. In accompanying us, they sometimes shot ahead and at other times loitered behind, as suited their plans. The stories they gave out among the unsuspecting and credulous natives, as they passed, were well calculated to astonish as well as attract attention. Brought up, as they had been near the whites —who rove, trap, and trade in the wilderness —they were capable of practicing all the arts of well instructed cheats; and to effect their purpose the better, they showed the Indians an old letter, and told them that they had been sent by the Great White Chief, with a message to apprise the natives in general that gifts, consisting of goods and implements of all kinds, were forthwith to be poured in upon them; that the Great White Chief knew their wants, and was just about to supply them with everything their hearts could desire; that the whites had hitherto cheated the Indians, by selling goods, in place of making presents of them as directed by the Great White Chief. These stories, so agreeable to the Indian ear, were circulated far and wide, and not only received as truths, but procured so much celebrity for the two cheats that they were the objects of

attraction at every village and camp on the way: nor could we, for a long time, account for the cordial reception they met with from the natives, who loaded them for their good tidings with the most valuable articles they possessed — horses, robes, leather, and Higaus; so that on our arrival at Oakinackin they had no less than twenty-six horses, many of them loaded with the fruits of their false reports.

At the Great Cascades, Thompson had to calm the natives' fears that the Astorians were bringing more smallpox. (The British and Americans, of course, accused each other of bringing diseases to the Indians. One Astorian even carried around a bottle, a "phial of wrath," which he said contained smallpox; he used it to threaten the tribes.) Thompson portaged his light canoes without incident, but the Astorians, loaded down with heavy dugouts and huge packages of trade goods, had trouble. Alexander Ross wrote:

Here the Indians crowded about us in fearful numbers, and some of them became very troublesome. A small present being made to each of the chiefs. They then pointed across the portage, or carrying place, as much as to say, "All is clear; pass on."

From this point we examined the road over which we had to transport the goods, and found it to be 1450 yards long, with a deep descent near the Indian villages, at the far end, with up–hills, and down–hills, and side hills most of the way. To say that there is not a worse path under the sun would be going a step too far, but to say that for difficulty and danger few could equal it, would be saying but the truth. Certainly nothing could be more discouraging than our present situation: obstacles on every side, by land, by water, and from Indians, all hostile alike. Having landed the goods and secured the canoes, we commenced the laborious task of carrying, and by dividing ourselves in the best possible manner for safety, we managed to get all safe over by sunset. Not being accustomed myself to carry, I had, of course, as well as some others, to stand sentinel; but seeing the rest almost wearied to death, I took hold of a roll of tobacco and after adjusting it on to my shoulder, and holding it fast with one hand, I moved on to ascend the first bank; at the top of which, however, I stood breathless, and could proceed no farther. In this awkward plight, I met an Indian and made signs to him to convey the tobacco across, and that I would give him all the buttons on my coat, but he shook his head and refused. Thinking the fellow did not understand me, I threw the tobacco down, and pointing to the buttons one by one, at last he consented, and off he set at a full trot and I after him; just as we had reached the camp at the other end, he pitched it down a precipice of two hundred feet in height, and left me recover it the best way I could. Off I started after my tobacco, and if I was out of breath after getting up the first bank, I was ten times more so now. During my scrambling among the rocks to recover my tobacco, not only the wag that played me the trick, but fifty others, indulged in a hearty laugh at my expense; but the best of it was, the fellow came for his payment, and wished to get not only the buttons, but the coat along with them. I was for giving him — what he richly deserved — buttons of another mould, but peace in our present situation was deemed the better policy; so the rogue got the buttons and we saw him no more.

All the Indians we saw about this place were in small camps or villages, and might number 250 or 300. They called themselves Cathleyacheyachs, and we could scarcely purchase from the lazy rascals fish and roots enough for supper. In dress, appearance, and habits they differed but little from those around Astoria, but the spoke a different language, although many of them understood and spoke [lower] Chinook also.

At first we had formed a favorable opinion of them; but their conduct soon changed, for we had no sooner commenced transporting our goods than they tried to annoy us in every kind of way —break our canoes, pilfer our property, and even threaten ourselves, by throwing stones and pointing their arrows at us. We were not, however, in a situation to hazard a quarrel with them, unless in the utmost extremity; and it certainly was with great difficulty, and by forbearance on our part, that we got so well off as we did. After finishing the labor of the day, we arranged ourselves for the night. The Indians all assembled again about our little camp, and became very insolent and importunate; they looked at everything, and coveted all they saw. Indeed, we were afraid at one time that we would have to appeal to arms; but fortunately, after distributing a few trifling presents among the principal men, they smoked and left us, but we kept a constant watch all night.

On the 29th, early in the morning, we prepared to leave the Cascades; but the bank being steep and the current very strong where we had to embark, we did not venture off before broad daylight, and before that time the Indians had crowded about us as usual. Their pilfering propensities had no bounds . . . notwithstanding all our care and kindness to them, they stole our canoe–axe and a whole suit of clothes, excepting the hat, belonging to Mr. McLennan, which we were unable to recover. We had no sooner embarked, however, than Mr. McLennan, in his usual good humor, standing up in the canoe and throwing his hat amongst them, said, "Gentlemen, there's the hat; you have got the rest; the suit is now complete," and we pushed off and left them.

A Nor'Wester trader, Alexander Henry the Younger, speculated on the cause of the hostility at the Great Cascades:

At the Grand Rapids the Indians seemed friendly; indeed at every camp where our people had communication with the natives, the latter appeared friendly; this shows them to be treacherous. They dared not attack us openly in their present

Voyageurs poling their bateaux past Beacon Rock. From Sam Lancaster's book on the Scenic Highway.

naked state, for want of firearms; they dread our guns. They have had war among themselves in the interior, and many have fled to the Columbia for safety and in readiness to escape across the river if pursued by their enemies, who, it seems have firearms. These villains, we are told, are bent on taking revenge upon us for furnishing firearms to their enemies above; and this is the reason why they are collected along the river in such unusual numbers.

The party intended to make the best of their way on, keep a good lookout, and camp in places where the Indians could not surprise them. The sight of the gun cases, we fear, may tempt the natives to be troublesome, and even desperate to get possession of them, as they know only firearms can put them on an even footing with their enemies; plunder seems to be their main object, not blood.

According to Alexander Ross, some conflicts were the result of misunderstandings about protocol:

Had they the moment the Indians threatened tribute, instead of paddling up in the middle of the stream stopped and made for shore, held out the hand of friendship, and smoked a pipe or two of tobacco with them there would have been an end to it, the affair would have been settled. This was the tribute the natives expected but the whites set the Indians at defiance by trying to pass them in the middle of the stream.

Ross, noting the many wrecked boats at the Great Cascades and the large amounts of goods lost when boats overturned there, complained that "we have never yet once been able to pass this Charybdis without paying tribute either to the natives or the whirlpools." The most common payment to the Cascade Indians was a few charges of "powder

Alexander Ross.

and ball" for each helper. David Thompson wrote about the portage residents:

We hardly knew what to make of these people; they appeared a mixture of kindness and treachery; willingly rendering every service required and performing well what they undertook, but demanding exorbitant prices for their services, and dagger in hand ready to enforce their demands.

The U.S. initiated transcontinental mail service to Fort Astoria in 1813, but the carrier, John Reed, was robbed of the mail in the Gorge. Descending the Gorge in the winter of 1813-14, Ross again had trouble at the place Washington Irving called "the piratical pass of the river":

On our way down the Columbia such was the mildness of the winter that not a speck of ice was to be seen. At the head of the Cascades, a place always notorious for its bad population we encamped, and were disturbed all night by the whooping and yelling of savages, who kept prowling in the woods around us. Notwithstanding the strictest watch, several arrows were shot into our camp and a man named Plessis was wounded in the ear. We fired several shots into the woods from a three pounder, which kept the Indians at a distance. In the morning we passed the Cascades peaceably.

Below the Cascades there is no impediment whatever to navigation of the river, by night or day. The brigade, therefore, went sweeping down the current in the dark. Next morning at daybreak, we met, opposite to the Wallamitte, two North-West canoes and twenty men, under the direction of Messrs. Keith and Alexander Stuart, two partners of the North-West Company, on their way to the interior. We breakfasted together, and I strongly advised them to turn back, since so small a party could never hope to pass through the hostile tribes in safety. They, however, made light of the matter, giving me to understand that they were North-Westers! so we parted, and they proceeded. While talking on the subject of danger, one of those swelling fellows, such as may be ordinarily seen stuck up in the end of a North-West canoe, with a bonnet of feathers surpassing in size the head of a buffalo bull, turned round to my men and said, "Do you think we are Americans? We will teach the Indians to respect us."

The Nor'Westers' bravado proved unfounded; they, too, were attacked at the Great Cascades. All their trade goods for the coming year were taken, and one man was hit with a poisoned arrow. He survived, thanks to an Iroquois trapper who sucked the venom out of the wound. A party of reinforcements rescued the men but had to retreat without recovering the trade goods. Ross gloated that the attack "taught the strutting and plumed bullies of the north that, although they were North-Westers, the lads of the cascades did not respect their feathers."

Gabriel Franchère.

However, this outright robbery was an unacceptable affront to the men at the fort; besides, the Astorians knew that the captured booty included 50 guns. Something had to be done. A large force was assembled that included warriors from lower Chinook tribes that were feuding with the Cascade Indians. The expedition headed up the river; when it reached the Cascades, however, nothing happened. The situation remained a standoff until, on the advice of their Indian allies, the white men captured important prisoners and held them hostage on Bradford Island. Threats to kill the prisoners and torch the villages were dramatized by military parades and a show of fireworks — which especially alarmed the Cascade Indians. The plan worked; the guns and some of the stolen goods were recovered without further bloodshed.

On the way back to the fort, the expedition stopped at "the Soto Village" to demand the remaining missing goods. Alexander Henry recorded the response:

The women came over with a few trifles, and told us they could get nothing more. However, we sent Casino with Mr. Franchère and a party of armed men to harangue the village once more, while we breakfasted on lean horse meat and fat seal, after which not a mouthful of anything remained for 70 persons, and there was no hope of a supply from the natives. Mr. Franchère returned with their answer, which was that we must be a bad lot to want all our property back after killing two chiefs, and they would give no more.

When the news of the War of 1812 finally reached the Northwest, Astor's partners, already besieged with troubles, were "persuaded" to sell out to the rival Canadian Northwest Company. Fort Astoria was renamed Fort George, and the new flagpole was christened with a bottle of Madeira. Most of the post's employees stayed on since they were originally Nor'Westers who had only recently been hired away by Astor. The local natives, however, were confused by the sudden change of flags and allegiances. When the British navy arrived to capture the fort from the Americans, its commander, Captain Black, was sad to learn that it had already changed hands peacefully. He was also unimpressed by the fort itself, complaining: "Why, is this the fort that was represented to me as so great? Good Lord, I could knock it over in two hours with a four-pounder!"

The Northwest Company built Fort Walla Walla (Nez Perce) east of the Gorge in 1818, the same year the U.S. and Britain signed a treaty for the joint occupation of the Northwest. Spain and Russia soon abandoned their claims to the wild region.

The British finally restored peace in the Gorge, their crucial trade route, crediting trader Donald McKenzie's "conciliatory yet firm and judious conduct" and promises of a more mutually-beneficial relationship. Alexander Ross, a veteran of earlier skirmishes at the rapids, was trapped at the Great Cascades by ice in 1816 with a large, vulnerable cargo. Fearful at first, Ross soon learned that times had indeed changed:

We soon learnt, however, that McKenzie was at home. His party consisted of about forty men, such as they were, retaining therefore a certain number about himself and the property, he adopted the new measure of distributing the remainder in the houses of the different great men among the natives apparently as boarders but in reality as spies; so that every hour he had ample intelligence of all that passed in the respective villages or camp. The chiefs were flattered by this mark of his consideration. They were no less pleased with the trifles which from time to time they received in payment, and all the natives of the place became in a couple of months perfectly familiarized with the whites.

A great deal of information was collected from these people, considerable furs also, and altogether such a footing established among them as promised fair to be turned to advantage in time to come. The chiefs were no less pleased to see McKenzie than anxious to know the cause of his return to their country. And he was greeted with a hearty welcome from all classes.

"We are rejoiced," said an old chief to him one day, "to see one of our first and best friends come back again to live among us. We were always well treated by our first traders, and got plenty of tobacco to smoke. They never passed our camp without taking our children by the hand and giving us to smoke, and we have always been sorry since you left us. Our traders nowadays use us badly, they pass up and down the river without stopping. They never take our children by the hand, nor hold out the pipe to us. They do not like us. Their hearts are bad. We seldom go to see them. Are you," continued the chief, "going to remain long with us?" McKenzie consoled the friendly old man, and told him that he would be long with them to smoke and take their children by the hand, and would never pass nor repass without giving them a smoke as usual. At these words, the chief exclaimed, "Haugh owe yea ah! Haugh owe yea ah!" These exclamations of gratitude showed that McKenzie was perfectly at home among them. Every countenance he met smiled with contentment, and his authority was as much respected by the Indians as by his own people, so that he considered himself as safe and secure in the Indian camp as if he had been in his own house. Nor had he sooner laid himself up in ordinary among the great Nabobs of the Cascades, than he was invited from wigwam to wigwam to partake of their cheer.

The Northwest Company dominated the Northwest fur trade until 1821 when Britain, in an effort to end increasingly violent competition, merged the company into the Hudson's Bay Company. Four years later the center of operations was moved upriver to Fort Vancouver; Dr. John McLoughlin became the Chief Factor. In 1828 the Hudson's Bay Company closed its small trading station at The Dalles; the Wasco Indians were so outraged that they sent a huge war party down to sack Fort Vancouver. McLoughlin learned of the raid and recruited 30 canoes of warriors from Chief Cassino of the Multnomahs. The Wascos were so impressed by the Hudson's Bay Company's defenses that they returned home—after watching a young Scot named Colin Fraser parade around the fort in kilts, blowing a bagpipe.

Dr. John McLoughlin.

Americans found the Hudson's Bay Company "all grasping." From Fort Vancouver, Quebec-born Dr. McLoughlin ruled most of the Northwest with a firm but generally fair hand. The worst sin a trading post could commit was "eating gold," expensive European provisions, but this was not a problem at Fort Vancouver, where the fertile soil grew so many apples—like "onions fastened in rows on a string"—that the limbs had to be supported with posts. A fishery was established at the Cascades. Missionary Narcissa Whitman called the post "the New York of the Pacific Ocean," and McLoughlin's empire extended as far as Alaska, where he traded dairy products to Russians.

Fort Vancouver's stockade was surrounded by farms and the homes of its employees, who included French-Canadians, Kanakas (Hawaiians), half-breeds, Iroquois Indians from the East and local Indians. The French-Canadian voyageurs were mainstays of the fur trade and generally felt more at home with the Indians than with the English noblemen. The voyageurs collected the furs, canoed them up the Columbia and carried them east, portaging their canoes and ninety-pound packs around the Great Cascades, the Narrows and Celilo Falls. Like the Cascade Indians, the voyageurs portaged the loads on their backs, supported by wide straps across their foreheads. When not trapping, they congregated around the fort, beating insects and dirt from furs and doing other odd jobs for the Company. Many of them, with their Indian wives, later settled across the river at French Prairie.

The Kanakas (or Owhyees) were recruited from the Sandwich (Hawaiian) Islands for a few years of hard work. Some of the Hawaiians came to stay and use their boating skills. One group of Hawaiian men settled east of Stevenson, near the mouth of Kanaka Creek, with their Indian wives and earned a living sailing cord wood up to The Dalles. The increasing number of white settlers often accused Kanakas of taking too many jobs; employers had to pay an annual tax on Hawaiian employees. Some of the men of the Kanaka Creek colony ended up moving to the Yakima Reservation when their wives were sent there.

The fur trading posts were company towns. The trappers, white or Indian (and often mixed), soon fell in debt for their provisions, a cycle hard to escape. More and more white trappers had to be brought in as Indian populations declined. In addition, many Indians, with their "natural indolence," didn't care to work for the Company. The head of the Hudson's Bay Company complained that "the Indians cannot be prevailed upon to exert themselves in hunting; they are independent of

us requiring but a few of our supplies and it is not until absolutely in need of an essential article or an article of finery such as Guns and Beads that they will take the trouble of hunting." A visitor to Fort Vancouver, Anglican Reverend Herbert Beaver, noted that: "Of articles bartered by the Company for peltry and other native produce, one half may be classed as useless, one quarter as pernicious, and the remainder of doubtful utility." The Hudson's Bay Company blankets, however, were very desirable.

The Chinooks much prefered trading to trapping, and they jealously protected their middleman role, sometimes by telling inland tribes that the white traders were cannibals. As fewer and fewer Indians brought beaver pelts to the posts, the white trappers were forced to go up the tributaries themselves; the life expectancy of these "free trappers" was short. Many, especially the American loners, married native women and lived more like Indians than like their white contemporaries. It was boom or bust, and danger was seldom far away; 500 American trappers perished in a little more than a decade. The motto of the Hudson's Bay Company became *pro pelle cutem* — "risk one's skin for a skin."

John Jacob Astor lost out to the British in the Northwest, but he tightened his grip on the Great Lakes fur trade. By 1834 he controlled trade as far as the Rockies, where General William Ashley's company had paved the way for the Oregon Trail. Fur traders from the U.S., having trapped out the beaver east of the Stony (Rocky) Mountains, now roamed over the Continental Divide in increasing numbers and began to threaten the British monopoly. The Americans, including Jedediah Smith, sent back glowing reports of the "Oregon Country." The Hudson's Bay Company attempted to stave off competition by trapping out all of the beaver along the Snake. The head of the company, Sir George Simpson, reasoned that: "While we have access thereto, it is our interest to reap all the advantages we can for ourselves, and have it in as bad a state as possible for our successors." Simpson considered the American trappers, "generally speaking, people of the worst character, run aways from jails and outcasts from Society [who] acknowledge no master, will conform to no rules or regulations." In 1836 Simpson imported a paddlewheel steamer, the *Beaver,* from England to the Columbia; he hoped to discourage the American ships (that traded as far upriver as The Dalles), but his ship used so much fuel that it was usually sailed.

Back in the U.S.A., expansionism and a religious revival increased pressure to colonize the Northwest and to bring salvation to its native population. The self-righteous leader of this crusade was a Boston schoolteacher named Hall Jackson Kelley; he demanded that Congress claim title to the Northwest and then grant his organization 100 miles of land along the lower Columbia. In exchange, Kelley promised to lead at least 3000 Americans west to establish a colony that would be "planned by Providence, made easy by Nature." Kelley even made a map showing the Willamette Valley subdivided into 40-acre tracts. The British, of course, would have to leave—they were corrupting the Indians.

Without a land grant and with only a few recruits, Kelley finally set out for the Columbia—via New Orleans and Mexico—only to arrive in California broke and alone. He finally reached Fort Vancouver in 1834 —in the company of horse thieves; McLoughlin shipped the indignant Kelley back to the U.S., where he became more fervent than ever.

Kelley's most important convert was Nathaniel Wyeth, a young Boston entrepreneur who had amassed a fortune shipping New England ice to the West Indies and Africa in antiquated whaling ships. Wyeth formed the Oregon Colonization Society and in 1832 set out across the continent to succeed where Astor had failed. He planned to establish an agricultural and salmon-pickling settlement on the lower Columbia that would also be the center for a fur trapping enterprise. He sent a supply ship around the Horn, but it wrecked. Wyeth finally reached the Columbia, but only after half his employees deserted him at a rendezvous near the Tetons. Without supplies, Wyeth had to return to the U.S.; but most of his remaining employees stayed at Fort Vancouver and settled down.

Two years later, Nat Wyeth tried again. Thinking that he had a firm contract to supply trade goods to trapping companies at a rendezvous, Wyeth arrived to discover that he had been beaten out by a rival; he had to build Fort Hall on the Snake River to unload the goods. Wyeth continued on down the Columbia and finally built his dream-post, Fort William, on Wappato (Sauvie) Island—across from the Hudson's Bay Company's Fort Vancouver. This time his supply ship did arrive, but too late for him to take advantage of the annual salmon runs. Wyeth's employees were "sick and dying off like rotten sheep of billious disorders," and the Hawaiian workers he imported deserted. Fourteen of his men were killed in the mountains by natives. The local tribes were reluctant to hunt or fish for him; they feared the British—and blamed the Americans for the devastating diseases. Wyeth was defeated a second time, so he sold out to McLoughlin and returned to the U.S. to resume the life of a rich Massachusetts ice merchant.

Wyeth had come to the right place at the wrong time. The fur trade was dying as the beaver disappeared and fashion turned from pelts to silk. Finally, he was not powerful enough to challenge successfully the Hudson's Bay Company monopoly. However, the missionaries Wyeth brought with him on the second trip succeeded where he failed. Although there were few natives left to "save," the missionaries stayed anyway and helped to bring the Oregon Country into the U.S.A.

Nat Wyeth.

Most newcomers were motivated by monetary gain, but a few people visited the Northwest to study its remarkable flora and fauna. David Douglas, a Scottish botanist, was commissioned to study Northwest flora by the Royal Horticultural Society of London while still in his twenties. Douglas first came to the lower Columbia aboard a Hudson's Bay Company ship in 1825; he quickly took to the wilderness and would leave the British outposts for months at a time to wander alone. Carrying a heavy pack of plant-collecting equipment, Douglas could still cover 50 miles a day. He depended upon his gun for food—except for tea, which he carried in a tin—and usually slept on pine or fir boughs.

Douglas became famous among the Indians as the "Grass Man," a reference to his tireless plant collecting; his reputation as a great marksman also spread fast. He carried a magnifying glass to light his pipe, and it amazed the natives, as did his eyeglasses. Whenever Douglas put on his spectacles, the natives would clasp their hands over their mouths, their sign of astonishment or dread. He once took out his razor and shaved Chief Comcomly's brother, Tha-amu-u, "The Beard," so that he could look like a "King George Chief." Douglas claimed to be the first white man to visit the Cascades "without guard," but at Celilo Falls, he had to be rescued from hostiles by a band of Cayuse, who were then still friendly to the newcomers.

Douglas' stamina was amazing. He once climbed for three days up the north wall of the Gorge to the crest of the Cascade Mountains (which he named for the Gorge's rapids); his guide, Chief Chumtalia, faked sickness rather than try to keep up with the crazy Grass Man. The next day, the botanist climbed for fifteen hours up the south escarpment to the summit, where he found the noble fir and the Douglas fir (which was named in his honor). He found one fallen Douglas fir that was 227 feet long and over 15 feet in diameter.

Douglas explored the Northwest for two years, traveling over 7000 miles, before he sailed back to England. He soon bored of "civilized" life, however, and returned to the Northwest wilderness. Douglas was killed in Hawaii in 1834; hiking along the rim of Mauna Kea, he fell into a pit trap for wild cattle. It was already occupied by a bull. He had brought hundreds of unknown plants to the attention of the scientific community, and British gardens are filled with American plants he introduced.

Physician/ornithologist John Townsend and botanist Thomas Nut-tall came to the Gorge in 1834 with Wyeth's second expedition and headquartered on Sauvie Island. Townsend, whose material was used by Audubon in *Birds of America,* was called the "Bird Chief" by the natives. He spent two years on the Columbia, working as a doctor part of the time, but mostly documenting the bird life of the Northwest. His detailed journal sadly described the depopulation of the Chinookan peoples.

David Douglas.

Beginning in 1829, a second epidemic, the "cold sick," swept through the natives along the lower Columbia, nearly extinguishing the survivors of the first plague. It is now generally believed to have been malaria from Fort Vancouver, although some think it was an Asian flu. The high death rate reflected the Indian's lack of immunities and the preferred treatment: a sweatbath followed by a plunge into the cold river. As purging as these primitive saunas may have felt, at least afterwards, they did more harm than good for malaria victims. In 1834 Townsend wrote:

The Indians of the Columbia were once a numerous and powerful people; the shore of the river, for scores of miles, was lined with their villages; the council fire was frequently lighted, the pipe passed round, and the destinies of the nation deliberated upon...Now, alas! where is he? —gone; —gathered to his fathers and to his happy hunting grounds; his place knows him no more. The spot where once stood the thickly peopled village, the smoke curling and wreathing above the closely packed lodges, the lively children playing in the front, and their indolent parents lounging on their mats, is now only indicated by a heap of undistinguishable ruins. The depopulation here has been truly fearful. A gentleman told me, that only four years ago, as he wandered near what had formerly been a thickly peopled village, he counted no less than sixteen dead, men and women, lying unburied and festering in the sun in front of their habitations. Within the houses all were sick; not one had escaped the contagion; upwards of a hundred individuals, men, women, and children, were writhing in agony on the floors of the houses, with no one to render them any assistance. Some were in the dying struggle, and clenching with the convulsive grasp of death their disease-worn companions, shrieked and howled in the last sharp agony.

Probably there does not now exist one, where, five years ago, there were a hundred Indians; and in sailing up the river, from the cape to the cascades, the only evidence of the existence of the Indian, is an occasional miserable wigwam, with a few wretched, half-starved occupants. In some other places they are rather more numerous; but the thoughtful observer cannot avoid perceiving that in a very few years the race must, in the nature of things, become extinct; and the time is probably not far distant, when the little trinkets and toys of this people will be picked up by the curious, and valued as mementoes of a nation passed away for ever from the face of the earth. The aspect of things is very melancholy. It seems as if the fiat of the Creator had gone forth, that these poor denizens of the forest and the stream should go hence, and be seen of men no more.

Townsend added that tribes that once struck fear into the hearts of newcomers had become "as submissive as children."

Rev. Samuel Parker, assessing the opportunities for missions in the Northwest, wrote:

I have found the Indian population in the lower country —below the falls of the Columbia —far less than I had expected, or what it was when Lewis and Clark made their tour. Since the year 1829 probably seven-eighths — if not, as Dr. McLoughlin believes, nine-tenths —have been swept away by disease.

So many and so sudden were the deaths which occurred that the shores were strewed with the unburied dead. Whole, and large, villages were depopulated, and some entire tribes have disappeared; but where there were any remaining persons they united with other tribes. This great mortality extended not only from the vicinity of the Cascades to the shores of the Pacific but far north and south.

It is hard now to fathom the horror of these plagues. The victims, watching their families and friends dying all around them, could not understand what was happening. Evil spirits might be responsible, but more likely it was the white newcomers, especially since the settlers had just started plowing Mother Earth. Many Whites felt that the epidemics were the work of God to remove "the chief obstruction to the entrance of civilization and . . . the introduction of Christianity." The gruesome scene was graphically described in *Bridge of the Gods*, a century-old "romance of Indian Oregon":

Through the hot months of summer the mortality continued. The valley was swept as with the besom of destruction, and the drama of a people's death was enacted with a thousand variations of horror. When spring came, the invaders entered the valley once more. They found it deserted, with the exception of a few wretched bands, sole survivors of a mighty race. They rode through villages where the decaying mats hung in tatters from the half-bare skeleton-like wigwam poles, where the ashes had been cold for months at the camp-fires; they rode by fisheries where spear and net were rotting beside the canoe upon the beach. And the dead— the dead lay everywhere: in the lodges, beside the fisheries, along the trail where they had been stricken down while trying to escape, — everywhere were the ghastly and repulsive forms.

The spirit of the few survivors was broken, and they made little resistance to the invaders.

"Cape Horn" from 1853-5 Pacific Railroad Report (by the Secretary of War).

6. Manifest Destiny

Indeed, I am fully convinced that when a people refuse or neglect to fill the designs of Providence, they ought not to complain at the results; and so it is equally useless to be anxious on their account. The Indians have in no case obeyed the command to multiply and replenish the earth, and they cannot stand in the way of others doing so.

— MISSIONARY MARCUS WHITMAN IN 1844

It is our manifest destiny to overspread and possess the whole of the continent which Providence has given us for the great experiment of liberty.

— NEW YORK MORNING NEWS EDITOR JOHN L. SULLIVAN IN 1845

Nationalism, expansionism and racism reached fever pitch in the middle of the 19th century. The United States righteously "annexed" the Texas, California and Oregon Territories and eyed the rest of the continent; the European powers had their hands full back home. A decade after the Great Pestilence, covered wagons began streaming into the Columbia Gorge, the last of the many obstacles along the Oregon Trail — and the worst.

Their tribes decimated, the Chinookan survivors drew together into a few groups for protection. My great-great-grandfather, Ta-hon-nah Tumalth, Kalliah's father, moved upriver from Wappato (Sauvie) Island to the Great Cascades, where a few hundred natives gathered; they became collectively known as the Cascade Indians. Their glory days were over, their traditional way of life in ruins.[21]

Many Cascade Indians retreated into a limbo world between cultures — trying to get along with ever-increasing numbers of white people, strangers they could not understand, while trying to salvage their heritage, their identity. Although cultures being forcibly extinguished don't always show their best faces, many Cascades were able to retain their pride.

Standing (from left): Mary Bradford-Wacomac, Maggie Wacomac-McLaughlin, Georgia Jackson, Alice Wacomac-Williams, George Foreman, Josie Korner, Henry Thomas, Joe Corner, Virginia Miller. Seated: Unknown woman and Wacomac. 1898 photo taken at the Cascades.

Wacomac, a Cascade Indian, had a pirate-style peg leg. He died during the construction of Bonneville Dam, still not believing that it would hold back the river. His daughter, Maggie McLaughlin, is alive and well (page 49).

Christianity spread through the tribes, and some Klickitats and Cascades became Catholics; but many of my ancestors despised missionaries, accusing them of patronizing—and even tricking—converts. Revivalistic religious movements—Shakers, Dreamers and the Feather Cult—flourished. These Longhouse Religions contained elements of Christianity and generally featured messiahs, who had died but later returned from the Land of the Dead to preach against evil. The Shaker Religion spread from Puget Sound and still has followers; a white observer noted that Shakers "are required not to swear, lie, steal, fight, kill, work on Sunday, gamble, use tobacco or whiskey, oppress anybody, or do anything they know to be wrong." The Feather Religion was begun by Jake Hunt, a Klickitat, and became popular at Spearfish, the Indian fishing community near the Wishram village site; its followers, like the Shakers, believed in faith healing.

The Dreamer Religion, based on a return to traditional ways and Earthmother, was especially popular east of the Cascades. Its followers believed that if they were spiritually and morally strong enough, the white people would disappear. The founder, a famed warrior named Smohalla, made no secret of his disdain for the immigrants' ambitious development plans and their European work ethic:

My young men shall never work. Men who work cannot dream; and wisdom comes to us in dreams. You ask me to plow the ground. Shall I take a knife and tear my mother's breast? Then when I die she will not take me to her bosom to rest. You ask me to dig for stone. Shall I dig under her skin for her bones? Then when I die I cannot enter her body to be born again. You ask me to cut grass and make hay and sell it and be rich like white men. But how dare I cut off my mother's hair?[22]

This lack of enterprise and ambition, as it was often described, no doubt further strained relations between the conflicting cultures. In addition, some white traders were happy to encourage dependence on guns, liquor and tobacco. Many Indians, especially "breeds" (or "bloods")—those of mixed white and red blood—adopted "American" ways, only to become landless and unhappy, outcasts from both societies. In spite of a law passed in the Washington Territory that forbade marriage between Whites and anyone more than half Indian, intermarriage was common and further diluted native cultures.[23]

Jake Hunt and Martin Spedis.

Jason Lee.

The Wascopam Methodist Mission was the first permanent white settlement in the Gorge, but a Scot, James Birnie, had previously operated a Northwest Company fur trading post at The Dalles for a short time. The Dalles, or Winquatt, is the only wide spot in the Gorge and was visited by many early explorers. A Wasco Indian went to Washington, D.C., with Lt. John C. Fremont in 1843 and returned a decade later, educated at white schools.

The wave of white immigration started slowly at first. Sending missionaries to the "pagan" Indians became a moral crusade after a few Nez Perce and Flathead chiefs (whose tribe didn't flatten their heads) journeyed to St. Louis to request missionaries. John Townsend, who was part of the Wyeth expedition that brought the first missionaries to Oregon, described them as "men of respectable standing in society, who have arrayed themselves under the missionary banner, chiefly for the gratification of seeing a new country, and participating in strange adventures." Minister Frederic Homer Balch, author of *Bridge of the Gods,* described Northwest missionaries as "stern Puritans whose idea of religion was that of a life-long warfare against the world, the flesh and the devil." Some missionaries assured the Indians that the federal government would pay for lands taken, which led to fights and evictions when the promised funds were not paid.

In 1834 Methodist Jason Lee began missionary work in the Willamette Valley. Two years later Dr. Marcus and Narcissa Whitman and Henry and Eliza Spalding came west, bringing the first wagon across the fur traders' route that was to become the Oregon Trail. The Whitmans established a Presbyterian mission, school and medical clinic among the Cayuse (Waiilatpu) and others near Walla Walla; the Spaldings established another mission among the Nez Perce to the east. Not to be outdone, Canadian Jesuits soon followed, causing bitter rivalries and much confusion among the natives interested in the newcomers' religion(s). Some missionaries even required native converts to pledge: "From this point on I will be a white man." Other natives often considered these Christian converts to be "low-class."

In general, Catholic priests in the Northwest were more tolerant of the natives' lifestyles; they were often willing to baptize and accept as Christians many Indians still considered "heathens" by Protestant missionaries. Catholic Iroquois Indians in the employ of the Hudson's Bay Company made many converts. Father Blanchet wrote about an 1841 evangelical visit to Tomaquin and the other converts at the Great Cascades:

I reached the camp of the idolators about 8 o'clock in the morning, armed with the token of our salvation. The good Tamakoun came before me to clasp my hand; the rest imitated him . . . Tamakoun, whose docility and confidence I wondered at, spent entire evenings talking about religion with me.

Blanchet admitted, however, that he had to make the rounds of the lodges every day because of "the indifference of a large number whom I was obliged to hunt up in order to bring them to the instruction." Missionaries often used a "ladder," a series of paintings of important Biblical events, to teach Christianity. James Swan wrote about finding a group of native children "playing priest"; a young boy was preaching in Latin (with a Chinookan accent) and baptizing the congregation's dolls.

In 1838 Jason Lee's nephew, Daniel, and a few helpers founded the Wascopam Methodist Mission at The Dalles. Daniel Lee labored there for five years, cultivating twenty acres before returning to the East. The Presbyterian Whitmans then purchased this shaky mission at The Dalles for $600; its only notable achievement had been an 1840 mass baptism of several hundred Indians after a week-long encampment near Chenoweth Creek. Many of these converts became discouraged when Christianity didn't improve their luck. The mission later became a U.S. Army post; only the stone monolith that served as a pulpit still remains.

Pulpit Rock and Rev. Joseph Luxello, a native convert and missionary. B. A. Gifford photo ca. 1896.

The trickle of immigrants on the Oregon Trail became a mass migration in 1842, and both the Waiilatpu and Wascopam Missions provided aid. When exhausted pioneers finally reached The Dalles, the end of the trail, their destination was near. But their problems were far from over. The fertile and depopulated Willamette Valley lay just downstream, but settlers first had to descend the treacherous rapids enclosed by steep canyon walls. Wagons were usually put on make-shift rafts at Rowena and floated down to the Great Cascades of the Columbia, often with tragic results. Until the steep Barlow Toll Road was built up and around Mt. Hood in 1855, the newcomers had only the choice of running the rapids or portaging through my ancestors' home. 24

The portage around the Great Cascades was not much of a thoroughfare. Townsend considered it the "most miserable of roads" when he had to hike it several times in the rain.

We had all to walk back along the circuitous and almost impassable Indian trail, and carry our wet and heavy baggage from the spot where the boats had been unloaded. The distance, as I have stated, was a full mile, and the road so rough and encumbered as to be scarcely passable. In walking over many of the large and steep rocks, it was often necessary that the hands should be used to raise and support the body; this, with a load, was inconvenient. Again, in ascending and descending the steep and slippery hills, a single mis-step was certain to throw us in the mud, and bruise us upon the sharp rocks which were planted all around. This accident occurred several times with us all.

Providing guide service and helping the pioneers transport their remaining goods around the rapids became sources of income for the Cascade Indians. According to Peter Burnett, who came west in 1843, the tribe's experience as traders was helpful:

These fellows appeared to understand their interests very well, and subserved them often with as much acuteness as thorough Yankees. Employ all, or none, was the word.

Sarah Cummins, a pioneer making the portage in 1845, was pleased with the help she received from my ancestors:

A camp was established and Indian carriers assisted in the work. They were paid wages but seemed to appreciate the food provided them and not one instance of dishonesty occurred. Father could speak enough of the jargon to make himself understood and they were careful and considerate helpers. Not one deserted the ranks.

My mother and Mrs. Welch and the children were compelled to walk five miles

or more around the portage. The Indian boatmen assisted the children in this long walk over the rugged ground and before nightfall were safely around the Cascades.

The Cascade Indians also rescued a missionary's wife whose boat had capsized, but some of the immigrants were beyond help. A pioneer "saw one man, the father of four children, lying on his back upon a rock, taking rain in his face, seemingly having given up all thought of manly struggle." Two British officers wrote to their superiors about the 1845 arrivals:

That the gentlemen of the H. B. Company have not exaggerated the lamentable condition of these emigrants on former occasions is evident by the appearance on arrival of this, said to be the most wealthy and respectable of all the former. Fever and sickness have made a fearful havoc among them, and many are now remaining in a helpless condition at the "Dalles" and the "Cascades." They report 30 men, women and children having died upon the journey.

These emigrants from the U.S. did not treat the Indians as fairly as the Hudson's Bay Company officials did; the pioneers' double-standard of justice especially outraged the natives. The Northwest Indians and the British fur traders had gotten along fairly well. They served each other's needs and seemed to understand each other. The British had been more concerned with collecting furs than saving souls or homesteading, but the new Americans—known to the Indians as "Bostons"—moved into the Gorge and the Willamette Valley and began farming and logging and demanding that the U.S. government force the British out. John Muir also commented on the white settlers in the Willamette, "the most foodful of valleys":

It was here that the first settlements for agriculture were made and a provincial government organized, while the settlers, isolated in the far wilderness, numbered only a few thousand and were laboring under the opposition of the British government and the Hudson Bay Company. Eager desire in the acquisition of territory on the part of these pioneer state-builders was more truly boundless than the wilderness they were in, and their unconscionable patriotism was equaled only by their belligerence. For here, while negotiations were pending for the location of the northern boundary, originated the celebrated "54° 40' or fight," about as reasonable a war-cry as the "North Pole or fight." Yet sad was the day that brought the news of the signing of the treaty fixing their boundary along the forty-ninth parallel, thus leaving the little land-hungry settlement only a mere quarter-million of miles!

The 1846 treaty with Britain determined the U.S.-Canada border, legitimized the American immigrants (though not, of course, to the natives) and, combined with the discovery of gold in California, greatly swelled the traffic on the Oregon Trail. Five thousand people traveled the trail in 1847. One of these wagon trains brought measles to the Whitmans' Waiilatpu Mission and natives began dying at a rate of five a day. Soon half of the Cayuse had died. Already alarmed by the seemingly endless numbers of whites shooting their game, trampling their meadows, claiming their camas prairies and burning their fuel, some of the Cayuse blamed the Whitmans for the deaths and killed them. The Protestants blamed the "permissive" Catholics for putting the Indians up to it, but the main agitator apparently had been Joe Lewis, a bitter half-breed from Maine who convinced some of the Cayuse that the Whitmans' medicine was actually poison and had caused the catastrophic deaths. [25]

Reverend H.K.W. Perkins, one of the missionaries at The Dalles, explained in a long and painful letter to Narcissa's sister that the murder was inevitable because of the Whitmans' arrogance toward the Indians and their obvious preference for more white immigration. The Whitmans had failed as missionaries, but they became the martyrs to the cause of westward expansion. Perkins noted that he differed considerably from most of the other missionaries:

As for myself I could as easily have become an Indian as not. I completely sympathized with them in all their plans and feelings. I could gladly have made the wigwam my home for life if duty had not called.

The U.S. troops that had been recruited for Oregon had been sent instead to fight Mexico, so the Oregon settlers had to form a volunteer army to punish the Cayuse offenders. The immigrants were furious that the federal government had abandoned them in their time of need, and recruits were offered the right to "colonize the murderers' lands." The governor instructed the volunteer troops not to harm the "friendly" Indians around The Dalles, which became the soldiers' main supply post. These tribes had engaged in a few skirmishes with immigrants, but relations had remained generally cordial. Most fights had been begun by a few hot-heads on each side.

In 1844 the Government Agent had offered a $100 reward for the capture of Cockstock, a Wasco chief who had raided Oregon City. Cockstock was shot and killed during an attempted capture, but two of his would-be captors were shot by poisoned arrows. James de Saule, a mysterious black cook from Peru who kept popping up in strange situations in the Northwest, was convicted of causing the trouble by cheating Cockstock; he was banished from the area. [26]

A few months before the Whitmans were killed, another fight had broken out around The Dalles between white immigrants and natives. Even the Oregon City newspaper, the *Spectator,* blamed the immigrants for starting this skirmish. But the murder of the Whitmans put the native peoples around The Dalles in a bind. One chief, Siletza, was robbed by the Cayuse for not taking up arms. The army moved his band downstream "for their own protection"—and to remove them from the temptation of joining the rebels. Rumors spread, giving the volunteer army great alarm, that all the tribes above The Dalles were joining the Cayuse; but the powerful Yakimas and Walla Wallas caught and hung one of the Whitmans' killers. [27]

After some fierce battles, the Cayuse War finally fizzled out with the capture and executions of some suspects. To prevent further hostilities, the governor asked the volunteer army to build a blockhouse at Upper Cascades. No blockhouse was built, but a few cabins were constructed and named Fort Gilliam after a hawkish army officer who shortly thereafter accidently shot and killed himself. [28]

The Regulator *wrecked in the Cascades, 1898.*

The murder of the Whitmans prodded Congress in 1848 to establish the Oregon Territory, the first formal territory west of the Rockies; it included the present states of Oregon, Washington and Idaho, plus parts of Montana and Wyoming. The long-awaited U.S. troops finally arrived the following year (although some drowned while attempting to run the Great Cascades, and the other party lost its horses on the Barlow Road). Land for the federal installation at Fort Vancouver was bought from the British Hudson's Bay Company, but the fort was built with difficulty; soldiers kept deserting to the California gold fields.

The 1850 Donation Land Claim Act allowed pioneers to claim title to as much as 640 acres per couple. Francis Chenoweth soon filed a claim and settled on the north shore of the Great Cascades; the following year he built the Northwest's first railroad. Only a mile long, it skirted the worst of the rapids on wooden rails; goods were portaged by mule-powered wagons, and passengers usually walked. The rails were later lengthened to six miles. Chenoweth's prices were very high, so a competing portage railroad was soon built by Colonel Joseph Ruckel on the south shore, from Cascade Locks to Eagle Creek. Other land claims along the Cascades were soon settled. Waucoma, the Place of Cottonwoods, now known as the Hood River Valley, was homesteaded by Nathaniel Coe and others after a hard winter drove out the first white settler.

Although Daniel Bradford, who ran the store at Upper Cascades, and others helped the desperate immigrants, some of the newcomers to the Gorge evidently treated those who followed them as badly as the Cascade Indians had treated early explorers. One pioneer wrote:

At the Dalles, the Cascades, and other points of travel, there were persons ready to take advantage of the pressing necessities of the emigrants, charging them enormous prices for everything, and for any assistance rendered. They were as bad as the pirates on the high sea, ready to prey on the sick or dying, willing to take the last dollar.

Rev. Ezra Fisher was also disgusted with the new residents at the Great Cascades of the Columbia:

I visited The Cascades, a town site, with eight or ten families scattered on the north bank of the Columbia for a distance of three miles from the head to the foot of the Cascade Falls.... These families have resorted here for matters of speculation and, with few exceptions, manifested less desire for the bread of eternal life than for the mammon of unrighteousness.

C. E. Watkins photo of the Oregon portage at the mouth of Eagle Creek.

Another C. E. Watkins photo of the Oregon Portage Railroad. Most of Watkin's Gorge photos were taken in 1867.

The introduction of steamboat travel further fueled speculation and price-gouging. The first steamboats began to ply the mid-Columbia in 1851, but the route upriver was interrupted by the Gorge's rapids and waterfalls. Steamboat passengers heading upriver from Oregon City to The Dalles had to portage around the Great Cascades and then catch another steamboat. The *James P. Flint* was the first steamboat on the Cascades-Dalles route, followed in 1854 by the *Mary* and the *Wasco*. Shipping freight was expensive — $75 per ton from Portland to The Dalles.

The steamboats each burned about four cords of wood an hour, and cutting firewood became a major source of income for the settlers of the thick forests around the Cascades. Even after steamboat travel began to wane, residents of The Dalles needed huge quantities for heating and cooking; their only alternative was to buy coal shipped by rail from Wyoming. In the 1860 s, wood bought for $1.25 a cord at the Cascades sold for $4.50 a cord at The Dalles. Flumes were built to float wood down to the river, and—as is happening again today—the forests above Stevenson were quickly denuded.

1514 - Steamer Landing, Hood River, Oregon.

Sail-powered scows were used to haul the firewood upstream to The Dalles; they often had to wait days — and sometimes weeks — for a favorable wind. With a good tail wind, the trip to The Dalles could be made in eight hours. The windjammers were 80-90 feet long, and some could carry more than 100 cords per trip. At The Dalles, the scows were beached, and horse-drawn wagons were driven into the river to unload the firewood. For the trip back downstream, the upper sail was thrown over the front of the scow. Bags of rocks tied to the sail pulled it down, making a "water-sail" to take advantage of the river's current.

The Dalles, then the end of the line for steamboat travel, was becoming one of the Northwest's major towns. Nathan Olney had opened a store there in 1847, a year before the St. Peters Catholic Mission was established. The U.S. Army declared a ten square mile military reservation — a controversial federal takeover — at The Dalles, and a rifle regiment from Fort Vancouver built a supply center there, Camp Drum. An outraged writer of an 1851 letter to the Salem newspaper,

Oregon Statesman, claimed that "this yoke of bondage" upsurped every possible boat landing and that "our place would improve and the country around would soon be settled, were it not for the encumbrances imposed by the military, which hang as dead weights to every enterprise." The military, however, encouraged settlement within its reservations because fewer soldiers would be needed. Even then, many land speculators were at work in the West; they convinced Congress to reduce the size of the original military reservations. The post at The Dalles was reduced to one square mile and would have been cut to twenty acres had it not undergone a quick change of name to *Fort Drum.*.29

The soldiers spent much of their time helping the immigrants who poured in on the Oregon Trail. In the fall of 1852, the commanding officer reported to headquarters:

About 1500 waggons or 6000 souls have arrived at this point this fall and about 600 more waggons are to follow. There is great suffering among the emigrants, mainly caused by the want of grass for their teams. Traveling in great crowds it has been destroyed by consumption, but especially by fires this side of Fort Hall. I have allowed the loan of 29 mules to be turned over to agents from Portland and other parts of Oregon, to transport flour and other provisions sent for distribution to suffering emigrants.

It is probable that I shall find it necessary to establish here for the winter a temporary hospital to shelter the sick among the emigrants who cannot get down the river and whose destitution is so great as to imperiously demand this aid. I trust that the General will order a medical officer to this post.

The post eventually became a refugee camp, and it employed many of the tired pioneers who were laying over for the winter.

By 1854 the settlers had ferries operating across the John Day and Deschutes Rivers. Some settlers began to cross the Deschutes at Buck Hollow in order to join the Barlow Road without having to pass through The Dalles. By this time, early skirmishes between pioneers and natives along the Oregon Trail foreshadowed battles that were to bring overland travel to Oregon to a temporary halt.

"Incidents" between natives and immigrants led to never-ending circles of reprisals. A separate Washington Territory, then with fewer than 4000 white residents, was carved from Oregon in 1853. The same year 150 Wishrams at the Narrows died of smallpox; the disease kept the other tribes from coming in to trade and ended the long trade mart tradition.

Ambitious young Isaac Stevens became Washington Territory's first governor and its Indian agent (supposedly representing the natives—an obvious conflict-of-interest). Stevens, who was also surveying for a railroad, set out on his own version of "shuttle diplomacy": a whirlwind tour of councils with Washington's many tribes. In 1855, he was able to pressure the major tribes into signing treaties that established reservations in exchange for seldom-kept promises of education, annual provisions and hundreds of thousands of dollars—in addition to assurances that the tribes would be left alone on their reservations. Most

Isaac Stevens.

natives on the Oregon side of the eastern Gorge were to be moved to the Warm Springs Reservation; those on the north bank were to go to the Yakima Reservation. As was common, different cultures—even rivals —were thrown together in landscapes foreign to many of them.

The government intended to convert hunter-gatherer peoples into farmers. Stevens addressed natives as "my children," which was not appreciated, and told them that they "must choose places in which to live, put fences around them, plow, and reap crops." By concentrating the reduced native populations into a much smaller area, Stevens opened large areas for more white settlers—and his own pet project, a railroad from Minnesota to Puget Sound.

White settlers soon violated the treaties, and Indian leaders became furious with Governor Stevens. Wagon trains were attacked, and terrorism by both sides increased. The natives soon realized that the U.S. government had no intention of keeping its promises (despite the good intentions of some of its representatives) and would not, or could not, keep white settlers from exploiting the remaining Indian enclaves. Coordinated battles broke out on several fronts in the Northwest. Stevens was blamed; he was smart and courageous, but his motives had been suspect from the start. General John Wool, head of the U.S. Army in the West, called him "crazy"; another contemporary claimed that "Governor Stevens was intoxicated and unfit for transacting business while making these treaties."

Stevens made many verbal promises, but often concealed the actual provisions of the treaties from their native signers. Owen Bush, one of Stevens' staff at the signing of the Medicine Creek Treaty with the Puget Sound tribes, refused to take up arms when the treaty later failed, explaining:

I could talk the Indian languages, but Stevens did not seem to want anyone to interpret in their own tongue, and had that done in Chinook. Of course it was utterly impossible to explain the treaties to them in Chinook. Stevens wanted me to go into the war but I wouldn't do it. I know it was his bad management that brought on the war, and I wouldn't raise a gun against those people who had always been so kind to us when we were weak and needy.

The leader and tireless organizer of the Northwest revolt was the famed Yakima chief, Kamiakan, who had once asked for missionaries and who had reluctantly signed a treaty at Walla Walla. It was illegal at the time to sell ammunition to Indians (which infuriated friendly tribes — who claimed that only "outlaw" Indians could obtain arms), but

Kamiakan had nonetheless accumulated an ample supply. Late in 1855, some Yakimas killed Andrew Bolon, a well-meaning Indian agent, and began attacking miners who crossed tribal land on their way to the Colville mines. Aided by the pro-war factions of some other tribes, the Yakimas then attacked a U.S. Army expedition near Toppenish; the soldiers were forced to retreat and to build a blockhouse on the Klickitat River. Volunteer armies were again raised; the so-called Yakima War had begun.

Kamiakan.

Peu-peu-mox-mox drawn by Gustavus Sohon.

The Yakimas and the Walla Wallas next captured Fort Walla Walla. The famed Walla Walla chief, Peu-peu-mox-mox, a long-time friend of Whites, was captured by the volunteer soldiers when he tried to negotiate a peace. He was killed, allegedly while trying to escape during a siege that lasted four days. The volunteers scalped Peu-peu-mox-mox, then cut the scalp into many pieces after displaying it; souvenir razor straps were cut from the skin of his back.[30]

The regular army often thought that the hawkish, land-hungry volunteers were more trouble than they were worth; the governors usually preferred the volunteers. General Wool opposed the use of volunteers in the Yakima War, believing that "their net result was to turn friendly and neutral Indians into hostiles." The killing of Peu-peu-mox-mox, whose Christian son had already been murdered by Whites, was a severe setback to peace. General Wool believed that settlers should keep out of the Indian country east of the Cascades, and he would not give supplies to the volunteer army that planned to winter in the Walla Walla Valley; the U.S. troops returned to The Dalles for the harsh winter. Colonel James Nesmith of the Oregon Mounted Volunteers bitterly wrote:

> This dammed war has got to be humbug . . . the Indians have run to Hell, or Texas, and our horses are too much broken down to persue them. . . I am satisfied that the best thing that could be done would be to recall the troops. Their suffering in the Yackama has been of the severest kind, and with a still worse prospect before them. There is now laying in the Garrison here about 450 regulars whose duty it is to protect settlers, they are in good quarters, while we poor devils tentless and otherwise destitute are by the Governor's orders to march to Walla Walla. God Dam such folly.

However, the hawkish Willamette Valley settlers wouldn't hear of such cowardice; the volunteers spent the winter in the field, where they pillaged missions and the settlers they were supposed to protect.

The U.S. Army's choice of The Dalles as its headquarters for the Yakima War meant that all supplies had to be portaged around the Great Cascades, a slow process that delayed needed provisions. On the north shore of the river, Whites had already built small settlements at each end of the Cascades; and a blockhouse, Fort Rains, was soon built on a point between them (just upstream from the dam). But the area was also settled by many Cascade Indians, including Tumalth and my Wish-ham great-great-grandmother and their four young daughters and baby son; they lived along the oxbow lake where the Bonneville substation is now located. Family tradition says that Tumalth also had three other wives.

Tumalth's village was at the upper end of Greenleaf Slough, the lake directly below Mt. Adams in the above photo taken from the summit of St. Peter's Dome.

Tumalth, as the "first chief" of the "Wah-lal-la band of the Tum-waters," had signed the 1855 Willamette Valley Treaty in which he and the other signers relinquished the south bank of the Cascades' territory but explicitly retained the north shore. (In other words, we Cascade Indians still own the Washington side of the Gorge as far as the Little White Salmon River.) The treaty, signed by Indian Agent Joel Palmer in Dayton, Oregon (where my mother's grandparents were among the early white settlers), established the Grand Ronde reservation; it no longer exists. The signers were promised food, clothing, wagons, cattle, horses and teachers, but they seldom received any of these payments. Though only in his mid-twenties, Tumalth was not to live long enough to be banished to the reservation near the coast.

Early in 1856, the Columbia Gorge was relatively calm, especially since a war was going on. The Cascade Indians still outnumbered the Whites around the portage — but obviously not for long. Tensions between the settlers and the natives was obvious, but on the surface it was business as usual. Construction was booming along the Great Cascades. One immigrant boasted he made more in one day as a shipbuilder at "Baghdad" (Upper Cascades) than the $8 a month he had made as a carpenter and mechanic back in Illinois.

On March 26, just as the U.S. Army troops were leaving The Dalles for their spring campaign to capture rebels, there were only nine soldiers left at Fort Rains. The Yakimas and their allies attempted to rid the Great Cascades portage area of white settlers. After burning the Joslyn house, the only white residence on the north bank near the White Salmon River, the attackers moved downstream to the Cascades. Lawrence Coe, one of a party trapped in the Bradford store at Upper Cascades by the attack, described his ordeal in a letter: [31]

On Wednesday, March 26th at 8:30 a.m., after the men had gone to their work on the two bridges of the new railway, the Yakimas came down on us. At the first fire, one of our men was killed and several were wounded. Our men, on seeing the Indians, all ran for our store through a shower of bullets; except three, who started down the stream for the middle blockhouse, distant one and a half miles. Bush and his family ran to our store, leaving his own house vacant. The Watkins family came into our store after a Dutch boy had been shot in the house. There was grand confusion in the store at first; and Sinclair, of Walla Walla, going to the door to look out, was shot in the head and instantly killed. Some of us commenced getting the guns and rifles from behind the counter. Fortunately, about an hour before, there had been left with us for shipment below, nine government muskets, with cartridges, boxes and ammunition. These saved us. Our men soon got shots at the Indians on the bank above us. I saw Bush shoot an Indian, the first one killed, who was drawing a bead on Mrs. Watkins as she was running for our store. He dropped instantly.

The Indians now returned in force to us; and we gave everyone a shot who showed himself. They were nearly naked, painted red and had guns and bows and arrows.... We then saw Watkins and Baily running around the river side towards the place where Finlay was, the Indians in full chase after them. As our own men came around the point in full view, Bailey was shot through the arm and leg. He continued on, and plunging into the river, swam to the front of our store and came in safely, except for his wounds. Finlay also swam across and got in unharmed, which was wonderful, as there was a shower of bullets around him. Watkins came

next, running around the point; and we called to him to lie down behind the rocks; but before he could do so, he was shot through the wrist, the ball going up the arm and out above the elbow. He dropped behind a rock just as the pursuing Indians came around the point; but we gave them so hot a reception from our house that they backed out and left poor Watkins where he lay. We called to him to lie still, and we would get him off; but we were not able to do so until the arrival of the troops —two days and nights afterwards. During this time he fainted several times from cold and exposure, the weather being very cold; and he was stripped down to the underclothes for swimming. When he fainted, he would roll down the steep bank into the river; and, the ice-cold water reviving him, he would crawl back under fire to his retreat behind the rock. Meantime, his wife and children were in the store in full view and moaning piteously at his terrible situation. He died from exhaustion two days after he was rescued.

The Indians were now pitching into us right smart. They tried to burn us out— threw rocks and firebrands, hot irons, pitchwood —everything onto the roof that would burn. But as the bank for a short distance back of the store inclined towards us, we could see and shoot the Indians who appeared there. So they had to throw from such a distance that the largest rocks and bundles of fire did not quite reach us; and what did, generally rolled off the roof. Sometimes the roof got on fire; and we cut it out, or with cups of brine drawn from pork barrels, put it out, or with long sticks shoved off the fire balls. The kitchen roof troubled us the most. How they did pepper us with rocks. Some of the biggest ones would shake the house all over.

There were now forty men, women and children in the house—four women and eighteen men who could fight, and eighteen children and wounded men. The steamer Wasco was on the Oregon side of the river. We saw her steam up and leave for The Dalles. Shortly after, the Mary left, also. She had to take Atwell's fence-rails for wood. Engineer Buckminster shot an Indian with his revolver on the gangplank, and little Johnnie Chance went climbing up on the hurricane deck, and killed his Indian with an old dragoon pistol; but he was shot through the leg in doing so. Dick Turpin, half crazy, probably, took the only gun on the steamer, jumped into a flatboat alongside, was shot, and jumped overboard and was drowned. Fires were soon started under the boiler, and steam was rising. About this time, Jessie Kempton, shot while driving an ox-team from the mill, got on board; also a half-breed named Bourbon, who was shot through the body. After sufficient steam to move was raised, Hardin Chenowith ran up into the pilot-house and lying on the floor, turned the wheel as he was directed from the lower deck. It is almost needless to say that the pilot-house was a target for the Indians. The steamer picked up Herman on the bank above. Iman's family, Sheppard and Vanderpool all got across the river in skiffs, and boarding the Mary, were taken to

C. E. Watkins photo of Ft. Rains, the middle blockhouse; the building below the fort is the saloon.

The Dalles.

So passed the day, during which the Indians had burned Iman's two houses, Bradford's sawmill and houses, and the lumber yards at the mouth of Mill Creek. At daylight they set fire to Bradford's new warehouse on the Island, making it as light as day around us. They did not attack us at night, but on the second morning commenced again as lively as ever. We had no water, but did have about two dozen of ale and a few bottles of whiskey. These gave out during the day. During the night, a Spokane Indian, who was traveling with Sinclair and was in the store with us, volunteered to get a pail of water from the river. I consented and he stripped himself naked, jumped out and down the bank, and was back in no time. We weathered it out during the day, every man keeping his post, and never relaxing his vigilance. Every moving object, bush, shadow or suspicious thing on the hillside, received a shot. Night came again; we saw Sheppard's house burn. Bush's house near by was also fired, and kept us in light until four A.M., when, darkness returning, I sent the Spokane Indian for water from the river; and he filled four barrels. He went to and fro like lightning. He also slipped poor James Sinclair's body down the slide outside, as the corpse was quite offensive.

The two steamers having exceeded the length of time which we gave them to return from The Dalles, we made up our minds for a long siege, and until relief came from below. The third morning dawned; and lo, the Mary and the Wasco, blue with soldiers, and towing a flatboat loaded with dragoon horses, hove in sight. Such a halloa as we gave! As the steamers landed, the Indians fired twenty or thirty shots into them, but we could not ascertain with what effect. The soldiers, as they got ashore, could not be restrained, and plunged into the woods in every direction; while the howitzers sent grape after the retreating redskins. The soldiers were soon at our doors; and we experienced a feeling of relief in opening them.

The Fort Rains blockhouse and the Lower Cascades settlement had been attacked at the same time. The settlers at Lower Cascades, having been warned by Indian Jack and other Cascade Indians, escaped by boat, hurrying downriver to Fort Vancouver for help; their buildings were looted and set afire. Sgt. Robert Williams was one of the soldiers in the besieged blockhouse:

I discovered that the Indians were preparing for mischief on the day previous to the attack. In passing each way by the Indian camp, my attention was particularly attracted at seeing Indians standing together in council, and dressed in warlike costumes, while some few were playing at a game outside. So I hurried back to the blockhouse with my utmost speed, and then told Sergeant Kelly and my comrades my suspicions. But, by reason of our belief in the strength of our position, we did not dread any danger from Indians, or even think any more about it.

When the attack was begun, nearly all of the detachment were scattered around the vicinity. My first feeling was that of indignation at such foolish conduct, thinking all the while that somebody was firing off their revolvers. But the cook quickly found out that it was no play, by seeing the door of the cookhouse riddled with bullets. He immediately gave the alarm by crying 'Indians'. McManus and myself were standing close together near the hills and timber which closely surrounded us in front; and then we beheld to our horror, the painted and half-naked savages, exultantly firing. McManus, who stood by my side, was shot in the groin. He died shortly after, in the army hospital at Vancouver.

My wounded comrade and myself lost no time in getting inside of the blockhouse. The incessant firing and racket of the Indians gave unmistakable warning of deadly danger to those of my comrades who were strolling around. They all got to the blockhouse in safety, excepting Lawrence Rooney, who was captured upon the hill while cutting wood. The two or three unfortunate families who were living close by the blockhouse ran to it for safety; but several were severely wounded in running the gauntlet. We have with us seven wounded and three killed. Among the latter was Mr. Griswold, who might have escaped his death but for his overconfidence in the friendliness of the Indians towards him.

On the morning of the attack, Sergeant Kelly sent one of the men, Frederick Bernaur, to the Upper Cascades for a canteen of whiskey. Unfortunately, the Indians had commenced their attack on the blockhouse before he returned, preventing him from getting back to us. They shot him through both legs. He managed, however, to get to the bank of the river, and there hide from sight. He fainted several times from loss of blood; but the whiskey he had in his canteen supported his strength. When night came, he left his hiding place and got in safely to the blockhouse.

The second day, the Indians were still besieging us, and thus preventing us from getting water, which by that time all of us greatly needed, especially the wounded. But close by there happened to be a saloon owned and kept by one of the Palmer brothers; who, with his brother, kept a store at the foot of the hill by the river bank. Luckily, they made their escape immediately after the Indians made the attack, locking the doors of both buildings before they left. My army comrade, Wm. Houser, suggested that somebody should be allowed to go to the saloon and get whatever they might find that would alleviate hunger and thirst. I seconded his motion. Sergeant Kelly then permitted him and me to go.

The door being locked, my comrade had to break it open with an axe. We procured a dozen bottles of English porter, one decanter of brandy, the same of whiskey and wine, and a small box full of oyster crackers. We failed to get water;

but the articles mentioned satisfied every requirement except surgical aid until we would get relief, which we knew was close at hand by hearing the Cascades. After that signal of relief, we all relaxed the ceaseless vigilance we had all the time kept for the purpose of allowing a portion of our guards to take a little rest and sleep.

Lt. Phil Sheridan, later a famous Civil War general, was sent up from Fort Vancouver with his dragoons to drive off the attackers and reclaim the portage area. He captured Tumalth in the process, but I'll let Sheridan tell his side of the story:

The Columbia River was very high at the time; and the water had backed up into the slough about the foot of the Lower Cascades to such a degree that it left me only a narrow neck of firm ground to advance over towards the point occupied by the Indians. On this neck of land, the hostiles had taken position, and I soon learned by frequent shots, loud shouting and much blustering; then by the most exasperating yells and indecent exhibitions, they dared me to contest.

After getting well in hand everything connected with my little command, I advanced with five or six men to the edge of a growth of underbrush until we reached the open ground leading over the causeway or narrow neck before mentioned, when the enemy opened fire and killed a soldier near my side by a shot, which just grazing the bridge of my nose, struck him in the neck, opening an artery and breaking the spinal cord. He died instantly. The Indians at once made a rush for the body; but my men in the rear, coming quickly to the rescue, drove them back; and Captain Dall's gun being now brought into play, many solid shot were thrown into the brush where they lay concealed, with the effect of considerably moderating their impetuosity. Further skirmishing at long range took place at intervals during the day, with but little gain or loss, however, to either side; for both parties held positions which could not be assailed in flank; and only the extreme of rashness in either could prompt a front attack.

On the morning of March 28th, the savages were still in my front; and, after giving them some solid shot from Captain Dall's gun, we slipped down the river bank; and the detachment crossed by means of the Hudson's Bay boat, making a landing on the opposite shore at a point where the south channel of the river, after flowing around Bradford's Island, joins the main stream. But an examination of the channel showed that it would be impossible to get the boat up the rapids along the mainland, and that success could be assured only by crossing the south channel just below the rapids to the island, along the shore of which there was every probability we could pull the boat through the rocks and swift water until the head of the rapids was reached, from which point to the blockhouse there was smooth water.

Before starting, however, I deemed it prudent to find out if possible, what was engaging the attention of the Indians, who had not discovered that we had left their front. I therefore climbed up the abrupt mountain side which skirted the water's edge, until I could see across the island. From this point I observed the Indians running horse-races and otherwise enjoying themselves behind the line they had held against me the day before. The squaws decked out in gay colors, and men gaudily dressed in war bonnets, made the scene most attractive; but, as everything looked propitious for the dangerous enterprise in hand, I spent little time in watching them; and, quickly returning to the boat, I crossed to the island with my ten men, threw ashore the rope attached to the bow, and commenced the difficult task of pulling her up the rapids. We got along slowly at first; but soon striking a camp of old squaws, who had been left on the island for safety and had not gone over to the mainland to see the races, we utilized them to our advantage. With unmistakable threats and signs, we made them not only keep quiet, but also give us much needed assistance in pulling vigorously on the tow-rope of our boat.

I was laboring under a dreadful strain of mental anxiety during all this time; for, had the Indians discovered what we were about, they could easily have come over to the island in their canoes, and by forcing us to take up our arms to repel their attack, doubtless would have obliged the abandonment of the boat; and that essential adjunct to the final success of my plan would have gone down the rapids. Indeed, under such circumstances, it would have been impossible for ten men to hold out against the two or three hundred Indians; but, the island forming an excellent screen to our movements, we were not discovered; and, when we reached the smooth water at the upper end of the rapids, we quickly crossed over and joined the rest of the men, who in the meantime had worked their way along the shore. We should be very thankful to the old squaws for the assistance they rendered. They worked well under compulsion, and manifested no disposition to strike for higher wages. Indeed, I was so much relieved when we had crossed over from the island and joined the rest of the party, that I mentally thanked the squaws, one and all. When crossing to the north bank, I landed below the blockhouse some little distance and returned the boat for the balance of the men, who joined me in a few minutes.

When the Indians attacked the people at the Cascades on the 26th, word was sent to Colonel Wright, who had already gone out from The Dalles a few miles on his expedition to the Spokane Country. He immediately turned his column back; and, soon after I had landed and communicated with the beleagured blockhouse, the advance of his command arrived under Lieut. Col. Edward Steptoe. I reported to Steptoe and related what had occurred during the past thirty-six hours, gave him a description of the festivities that were going on at the Lower Cascades, and also communicated the intelligence that the Yakimas had been joined by the Cascade Indians.

When the place was first attacked, I also told him it was my belief that when he pushed down the main shore the latter tribe, without doubt, would cross over to the island we had just left, while the former would take to the hills. Steptoe coincided with me in this opinion, and informing me that Lieut. Alexander Piper would join my detachment with a mountain howitzer, directed me to convey the command to the island, and gobble up all who came over to it. Lieutenant Piper and I landed on the island with the first boatload; and after disembarking the howitzer, we fired two or three shots to let the Indians know we had artillery with us, then advanced down to the island with the whole command, which had arrived in the meantime. All of the men were deployed as skirmishers, except a small detachment to operate the howitzer. Near the lower end of the island we met, as I had anticipated, the entire body of Cascade Indians, men, women and children, whose homes were in the vicinity of the Cascades.

They were very much frightened and demoralized at the turn events had taken; for the Yakimas, at the approach of Steptoe, had abandoned them as predicted, and fled to the mountains. The chief and head men put all the blame on the Yakimas and their allies. I did not believe this, however, and to test the truth of their statement, formed them all in line with their muskets in hand. Going to the first man on the right, I accused him of having engaged in the massacre, but was met by vigorous denial. Putting my forefinger into the muzzle of his gun, I found unmistakable signs of its having been recently discharged. My finger was black with the stains of burnt powder; and, holding it up to the Indians, he had nothing more to say in the face of such positive evidence of his guilt. A further examination proved that all the guns were in the same condition. Their arms were at once taken possession of; and, leaving a small force to look after the women and children and the very old men, so that there could be no possibility of escape, I arrested thirteen of the principal miscreants, crossed the river to the lower landing and placed them in charge of a strong guard.

The bloody three day battle was over. The Yakimas were pursued but not caught. A bungling bugle call tipped off a group of Indians about to be caught in a trap between Sheridan and Steptoe's soldiers. The Cascade Indians who were not arrested were put on an island and told they would be shot if they tried to leave. Now back to Coe's letter for the hanging:

The Indians whom Sheridan had taken on the island were closely guarded. Old Chenoweth, chief, was brought up before Colonel Wright, tried and sentenced to be hanged. The Cascade Indians, being under treaty, were adjudged guilty of treason in fighting. Chenowith died game; he was hanged on the upper side of Mill Creek. I acted as interpreter. He offered ten horses, two squaws and a little

something to every 'tyee' for his life, said he was afraid of the grave in the ground, and begged for his life, to be put into the Indian deadhouse. He gave a terrific warwhoop while the rope was being put around his neck. I thought he expected the Indians to come and rescue him. The rope did not work well; and while hanging, he muttered, "Wake nica quas copa memelous." He was then shot. The next day, Tecomeoc and Captain Jo were hanged. Captain Jo said all the Cascade Indians were in the fight. The next day, Tsy, Sim Lasselas and Four-fingered Johnny were hanged. The next day Chenoweth Jim, Tumalth and Old Skein were hanged, and Kanewake sentenced, but reprieved on the scaffold. Nine in all were executed. Banaha is prisoner at Vancouver, and decorated with ball and chain. The rest of the Cascade Indians are on [Bradford] island, and will be shot if seen off of it. Such are Colonel Wright's orders. Dow Watiquin, Peter, Hahooka John and Kotzue —maybe more —have gone with the Yakimas.

Sometime afterward, Nikatani, an old chief, told Col. Wright the "true" story of the attack. According to him, Kamiakan had pressured some Klickitats to help him convince the Cascade Indians to join forces against the white settlers. Most of the Cascade chiefs refused to cooperate, but some of the younger men joined up. Nikatani also claimed that Chiefs Chenoweth (We-la-wa) and Banahi joined the Yakimas and burned their own homes to prove to the soldiers that they too had been attacked by the "hostiles."

Throughout their lives, Kalliah (Indian Mary) and Tumalth's other daughters maintained his innocence. His oldest daughter, Whylick Quiuck, or Virginia Miller, who was nine at the time, claimed she was with her father when they had canoed upriver to Bradford Island to try to prevent the attack — and they were also attacked. According to his daughters, Tumulth had warned his white settler friends of the impending attack, and Sheridan, infamous for his anti-Indian sentiments, had wrongly accused Tumalth. Half a century later, Virginia Miller told her side of the story to photographer Edward Curtis:

Taimatas, a Klickitat chief, married Hwaiak, a sister of my father Tamahl; but he mistreated her, and she ran away and married a Cascade man. Just after she had borne a child, old Taimatas, her former husband, came down to the river village, beat her, and dragged her about, and both she and the baby caught cold and died. Tamahl swore vengeance, and went to the Klickitat camp. Taimatas commanded his son to conceal himself, but the chief himself did not flee, because he was a great medicine-man and thought nothing could harm him. However, Tamahl killed him, and this caused a feud that brought about the death of the Cascade chief.

Whylick Quiuck, aka Virginia Miller, by Edward Curtis.

After the outbreak in the Yakima country, emissaries from the Klickitat camp came to the Cascades and arranged a dance. Word was sent to Tamahl, who was in his winter camp near Vancouver, and he came up. During the night I awoke and saw seven men, including Ipia, a Klickitat noted for his cleverness and 'Pupu-maks-maks' [presumably Piopia-maksmaks, the Wallawalla]. They told my father that they had already killed many white people, and in the morning they were going to kill those at the Cascade settlements. They were dressed for war. They said they were going to dance in the house of Wapanaha, and invited him to attend. Acceptance would signify an intention to join in the proposed attack, and refusal would mean his death at the hands of his enemies, the Klickitat. So to everything he merely said, 'Yes'; but as soon as they had left he hurried his four wives, Kisanua, Komashin, Wabaidiu, and my mother Wadaigia, with their children to the river, and put them into canoes. Kisanua and two young slave men paddled quickly down to Fort Vancouver and warned the soldiers, while the others crossed to Bradford island. No valuables nor property of any kind, and but little food was taken.

On the following morning the chief's brother, Puhpuh, put out to the island and warned Tamahl that his enemies were coming to kill him. We slid down an almost perpendicular bank on the south side of the island, embarked, and paddled for the mainland on the south side of the river. Round the end of the island came a canoe with several men, including Wapanaha, Ipia the Klickitat, and three hired Hood River Indians, namely, Chinuahl, Kahlanut, and Aiataiat. The leaders were Wapanaha, who was actuated by ambition, and Chinuahl, who was acting for Taimatas, son of the slain Klickitat chief. They began to shoot, and bullets splashed around our canoe filled with women and children. Tamahl ran the canoe ashore, leaped out, and pushed it back into the current; for he knew that they would cease shooting when he himself was out of range. They stopped firing. Just then a steamboat appeared downstream, and they withdrew to the Washington shore for the fighting with the soldiers that was to follow. We went down the river to the landing, and my father met us there. A half-breed interpreter named Jack (I think he was a Spokan), who was then living among our tribe, came down with another man in a small canoe. He told the soldiers that Tamahl was responsible for the massacre, that he had furnished powder. There was color of truth in this, in that during the preceding night, before the outbreak, Wapanaha had come into our house in the absence of Tamahl and said to one of his wives, "We need powder; give me some." Fearful of refusing, she handed him some powder. Without investigation the soldiers handcuffed Tamahl and at the Upper Cascades they hanged him.

A remarkable incident lends credibility to her claim. After the attack, Tumalth's wife and daughters were evidently taken as slaves by Klamath Indians but were freed during an unrelated U.S. Army attack. They were then taken to Fort Vancouver where, in a gesture almost unknown on the frontier, some soldiers took up a collection of gold and gave it to Tumalth's oldest daughter for the wrong done to her father. The remaining family then moved upriver to my great-great-grandmother's Wishram village or the temporary reservation established between the White Salmon River and the Klickitat River.

Isabel Lear Underwood, the granddaughter of Chief Chenoweth and the daughter of one of Sheridan's soldiers, bitterly maintained Chenoweth's innocence:

My mother and my grandmother were members of the Cascade tribe. My grandfather, Chief Chenoweth, was a member of the Hood River tribe of Indians. When the Yakimas and Klickitats attacked the Cascades they escaped, and the Cascade Indians were left to bear the brunt of punishment for the attack. My grandfather, Chief Chenoweth, had saved Mr. Hamilton, for whom Hamilton

OREGON HISTORICAL SOCIETY

"On Klickitat River" by Edward Curtis.

Creek and Mt. Hamilton were named, from being killed by Indians. Chief Chenoweth and eight other Cascade Indians were hanged. Indians do not write history, and while the white man, at the time the incidents occur, may know the facts, the history is written by the white men, so the Indian side is rarely known or told. You will usually find that when a treaty is made with the Indians, the white men expect the Indians to observe it to the letter, while the white men observe the treaty if it is to their interest to do so; otherwise they will violate it. Naturally, the Indians are restless when no dependence can be placed on the word of the white men. If Indians wrote their side of the Indian wars it would frequently be found that they were caused either by the bad faith of the white men or by acts of aggression of the whites. When white men are killed there must be victims sacrificed to atone. Chief Chenoweth, though a friend of the whites, was a victim of the vengeance of the white men.

Mary Attwell, an early Cascade Locks resident whose cedar rail fence had fueled the ship *Mary* during the attack, concurred that injustice had been done:

Mum-shum-sie, wife of Chief Chen o wuth came to our house to warn us. She said, "Chief Chen o wuth wants me to tell you that some Yakima Indians are in our village. He told them to not go near your home or bother you, but he does not know if they can be trusted. He thinks that it would be best if you took your 3 boys and hid in the woods until they went by."

Roger was away, so I took the three boys, Eddy was 6, Celly 3, and James Fremont (Monty), 1 year old, we hurried across the field into a thicket. We could still see Mum shum sie walking back toward her home, when she darted into the tall hay and laid down out of sight. In a moment here came about 20 warriors not far from where we were hidden. They were not from our local village, were taller and all armed with guns. Celly wanted to talk, "What's at?" and when I held my hand over his mouth he cried. The strange Indians were talking among themselves so did not hear Celly, and they did not go to the house. If they had seen Mum shum sie they might have considered her a spy and punished her.

Chief Chen o wuth was a good man and this was the first time that we needed to leave our home. Over 300 Indians lived near our home and we trusted them and they trusted us.

Revenge for the attack was swift. The wife and six young children of Spencer, a friendly Cascade Indian, were strangled with rope; their white murderers knew that the family was innocent. Phil Sheridan, not known for having a weak stomach, called it "a most cruel outrage" and later wrote that "this dastardly and revolting crime has never been effaced from my memory."

Upper Cascades and Ft. Lugenbeel. C. E. Watkins photo.

Soon after the attack on the Portage settlements, Seattle was under siege by natives, including the Klickitats, but was rescued by Navy ships. Sporadic battles occurred between the Indians and the U.S. Army across eastern Washington during the next year; each side had its moments of glory, but the Yakimas and their allies were finally forced to surrender. Most of the important chiefs had been killed, and numerous warriors were hung as examples. Colonel Wright captured 800 Indian horses and shot them; Kamiakan fled and never returned to the Yakima Reservation.

The Yakima War could have been even more disastrous, but General Wool showed considerable restraint because he believed that the Indians were in the right — a minority opinion that stirred up resentment among other Whites. He had little sympathy for the age-old tactic of provoking attacks by trespassing, then — invoking patriotism — encouraging revenge by the friends and allies of the "victims." When General Wool was transferred in 1858, his successor won instant popularity by ignoring legalities and announcing that the supposedly closed lands east of the Cascades were now open for white settlement.

Blockhouses were built at the mouth of the White Salmon River and at "Des Chutes landing"; two more were later added at the Cascades, one at each end of the portage. The construction boom resumed. Fighting between the red and white people was to continue in the West for the rest of the century, but the short-lived rebellion in the Gorge was over.

The trend was clear in the Northwest: Manifest Destiny was to prevail. Hin-mah-too-yah-lat-keht, Thunder Travelling to Loftier Mountain Heights, the famed Chief Joseph of the Nez Perce to the east and member of the Dreamer Religion, summed up the situation with his usual eloquence:

The White men were many and we could not hold our own with them. We were like deer. They were like grizzly bears. We had a small country. Their country was large. We were contented to let things remain as the Great Spirit made them. They were not, and would change the rivers if they did not suit them.

7. Fishwheels and Locks

OREGON HISTORICAL SOCIETY

Cascade Locks and the Cascades. Cross & Dimmitt photo.

Then it may be asked, why did such men peril everything—burning their ships behind them, exposing their helpless families to the possibilities of massacre and starvation, braving death—and for what purpose? I am not quite certain that any rational answer will ever be given to that question.

—James Nesmith, part of the Great Migration of 1843

Motivated by courageous patriotism, by greed, by a fatalistic long-ing for adventure, by hucksters' propaganda, by the need to escape the law—or by the feeling that their lives just couldn't get much worse, the pioneers came west. Their coming proved disastrous to the Native Americans, and despite the boomtimes and the optimism of a new era, life was hard for these newcomers to the "wilderness."

Gaffing salmon at Celilo Falls, with one of the Taffe fishwheels in the background. Prentiss photo.

Upper Cascades and Fort Lugenbeel by C. E. Watkins.

C. E. Watkins photo of the sternwheeler Cascade *at the Lower Cascades portage landing on Hamilton Island, which no longer exists; it is now the bulldozed site of the new town of North Bonneville.*

Margaret Windsor Iman, who came to Upper Cascades in 1852, in time for the Indian attack, later wrote:

I was sick in bed with a small baby at the time of the massacre. In the excitement I was carried from my bed up the river about a mile to where there was supposed to be a skiff. The skiff had been taken over to the other side of the slough by a man named Herman, who died at The Dalles later; so Mr. Simeon Geil, who was at our place, ran the skiff over to where we were. As I was being carried into the boat, it was discovered that my little boy, two years old, had been left asleep in the bed. Mr. Geil, who was young and good on foot, ran back and got him. So you can see a part only of what I went through in those early days.

I think that day was the worst I ever witnessed on the old Columbia and there have been many, taking it all in all. I don't care to see any more of them — the roar of the small cannon at the blockhouse, the firing of guns, the dead and wounded, the war cries of the warriors in their war paint, the burning of buildings, with my

house among them, the fleeing of the people, and I being all but well. The splashing waters and bounding skiff did not add to a speedy recovery for me, but we landed on the Oregon shore safely and took the steamer Mary *for The Dalles.*

The horrors I went through during those early fifties would be unendurable to the women of today. The Indian trail passed close enough to my house that the stirrups of the warriors would drag on the rough board wall all night long. The trail was pretty much hidden by the wild rose bushes and buck brush and other small vegetation as well. Many times I have witnessed this when all alone at night, while my husband would be out late on some kind of business and would be detained. I'll tell you it was all but pleasant during those olden days of the early fifties.

Lieutenant Sylvester Mowry, equally distressed by life in the Gorge, described The Dalles as "a most desolate place, with nothing to recommend it except wolves, coy-otes, rattlesnakes and skunks." Other officers agreed; for them the post was "mentally as well as pecuniarily, a great trial." The bend in the Gorge was a "dreary, isolated spot, destitute of all that makes life agreeable." "God help them," remarked another officer, happy to be only passing through. But the so-called Yakima War put The Dalles on the map.

The Narrows (Dalles) by C. E. Watkins.

Mt. Hood and The Dalles from Rockland (Dallesport) by C. E. Watkins, 1867.

By the fall of 1856, The Dalles was "improving fast"; it had become a thriving community of 52 buildings, including six dry goods establishments, four boarding houses, two billiard saloons, three blacksmith shops, a meat market and a livery stable. It was incorporated in 1857 as Dalles City, a name derived from *Les Dalles,* the French-Canadian voyageurs' term for the Narrows. The U.S. Postal Service later changed the town's name so it would not be confused with Dallas, Oregon.

Wasco County was the largest in the U.S. when its boundaries were established in 1854 with The Dalles as the county seat. Wasco County stretched from the crest of the Cascades to the Continental Divide and included Sun Valley, Idaho, and part of what is now Yellowstone National Park. Seventeen counties have been carved out of only the portion now in the state of Oregon. The original courthouse, finished in 1859, still stands and is now a visitor center. Skamania County on the Washington side of the river also once stretched all the way to the Rocky Mountains.

The end of the Yakima War made life more pleasant at The Dalles; it became a favorite wintering spot for miners and soldiers. By 1858, a newcomer to The Dalles metropolitan area, Josiah Marsh, was able to send good news home to his father:

We have all had verry good health ever sence we have bin in oregon. I took a Claim the fall of 54 for three hundred and 20 achers of land. ther is a good grass Country all rond it, good range for stock. I have one hundred achers of crop in this year a bout 60 achers of oates and the rest is potatoes and unions and corn. I think at the least calculation that we will clear too thousant dollars this year.

Wages is 60 to 75 dollars per mounth and hard to get men to work at that price as ther is new gold mines discovered they ar cauld the fort Colvil gold mines. ther is thousands of miners going too the new mines all the time. they hav war with the indiians all the time there has bin a grate menny miners kild by the indiians there has bin war everry since the fall of fifty four all through oregon. I have left my claim several times on the account of the danger of bing massecred by the read devels ther is danger all the tim, but the whites ar getting to strong for them wher I live but they ar fighting on the frounteers all the tim.

my Claim that I live on is on the bank of the Columbia river six miles below fort dalles. the steames boates pass my hous everry day and ther is a grat menny sail boates passing all the tim A doctor Shaug sold his Claim for six thousand four hundred dollars it lay within too miles of fort dalles. good land that layes near market is verry high Gorg Snipes is my nearest neighbor; he is wroth som four or five thousand dollars. ther has bin no emagration since the fall of fifty five a cross the plaines to oregon on account of the indian wars . . . ther has bin a grat menny emagrants com to oregon by watter the last few years so if you ar bond to com my way that is by water and then you will have no indians to fight but my advis to you is to stay wher you ar. I do not think you would be sadisfid if you was to com to oregon becaus the one half of the peopel in oregon are not sadisfid.

Fort dalles is considerbel larger place than Agency Iowa was when I left and ten times the bisiness caried on at fort dalles as there was in Agency but as for society we have non here a tall everry body is grasping for a fortun but it is getting better than it was when I first com to oregon. I want you to understand that oregon is as rough a country as most enny outher country in the world but it is generally healthy all throgh; for stock it cant be beat, for sheep it will beat the world. I have seen the fatest mutton in oregon I ever saw in enny other Country. to take oregon as a fruit country it cant be beat. ther is a great quantity of fruit raised in oregon, it payes verry well. vegettables of all kindes sell at a good price cash up and no grombling. I can make five dollars here as easy as I could mak five centes in Iowa but I can spend it just as quick as I would five centes in Iowa.

The Dalles in 1864.

A letter printed in the *Oregon Statesman* in 1858 agreed that The Dalles was finally coming into its own:

[The Dalles] is a pretty good sample of California towns of its size of 1849 and 1850, both in appearance and in the character of no small portion of its population. That it is to be one of the important towns of Oregon there can be no doubt. It is the key to the whole upper country lying between the Cascades and the Rocky mountains, which must some day or other be settled. The buildings here are in the main of wood, and mostly of a cheap character. But, there are several fine blocks built of a species of sandstone which is found in exhaustless abundance within the limits of the town. There are also some good wood buildings here. Real estate is not high, but it is said to fluctuate considerably during the violent winds which sometimes prevail. Sporting seems to be an important feature of the business of the town. Tippling houses about every third door. Gambling houses seem well patronized. The garrison here bears witness to the efficiency, business character and good taste of Capt. Thomas Jordan, the Quartermaster, USA, at this post. The buildings, and all the improvements are of the best and most substantial character, and the garrison is said to be the most comfortable one on the Pacific.

The Surgeon's Quarters.

The importance of The Dalles was due to its strategic location, and Fort Dalles, the army post, was the center of its economic vitality (in addition to caring for destitute "illegal aliens"). Hostilities with the Indians brought more soldiers—and more civilians to provide the army with supplies. More white settlers meant more trouble with the Indians, which meant more soldiers, and on and on.

Fort Dalles' claim of being "to the Pacific slope what Fort Leavenworth is to the east slope of the Rocky Mountains in its military aspects" helped attract federal construction funds. Quartermaster Thomas Jordan decided that the fort needed a touch of "good taste," an ingredient usually missing in Army architecture. He and Louis Scholl rebuilt Fort Dalles in Andrew Jackson Downing's "Picturesque," an architectural style popular in the suburban East. Downing had come to architecture through landscape gardening and felt that residences should be practical and fit into the "adjacent scenery"; his "Picturesque" style was based

largely on English countryside cottages. An Army contemporary remarked that Jordan had transformed Fort Dalles from "the most unattractive on the Pacific" to one whose cottage-style officers' quarters were "for taste superior to those we have seen at any other post." Scholl, a well-educated banker's son who had fled a German revolution, called Jordan's house "a real beauty," Downing's "finest building"; nor was Scholl modest about the commanding officer's accommodations:

The surrounding rocky and desolate landscape has considerably changed. Wildcherry trees, planted with my own hand, grace the southern side. Rose bushes and currants, etc., at different intervals, are scattered over the landscape. The house itself is the finest in all Oregon. The spacious hall and a broad staircase are the first objects the eyes meet by entering through a solid oak painted door in the true Elizabethan style; the parlor to the left, with its bracketted ceiling and green marble mantlepiece, are fine specimens of workmanship. The dining room, with its folding doors to the parlor and part of the hall with beautifully painted ceiling in fresco, then the office to the right by entering the Hall and library are well suited for quarters for the Col of our 9th regiment. The carriage road 12 feet wide leads in a curve with a gentle acclivity on the lower side down the hill to the parade ground, which with its green sward of grass, sown last winter, gives our place a very fine appearance.

By 1858 the construction and supply business employed hundreds of civilians as teamsters, packers, herders, carpenters, painters, stonecutters, wheelwrights, blacksmiths, masons and general laborers; a labor shortage resulted. Lt. Derby had been ordered to build a military road on the Columbia's north bank to alleviate the portage problems that had hindered the army in the Yakima War, but his men kept deserting. The lieutenant protested bitterly that Scholl had "carried off" his workers to build the fort. Among Derby's many accusations was the complaint that Jordan's chief clerk had been expelled from a Portland hotel "in company with a notorious prostitute whom he represented to be his wife." Derby also had an "Indian scare," but it turned out to be drunken deserters. He eventually had to raise wages to $52 a month to compete with local farms.

Jordan evidently ran a tight operation; his efficiency and inventiveness offset much of the extra cost of "good taste," but the elaborate architecture evoked increasing criticism. After inspecting the post, Deputy Quartermaster General Thomas Swords reported back to headquarters:

In regard to the building operations, I regret that I cannot speak even so

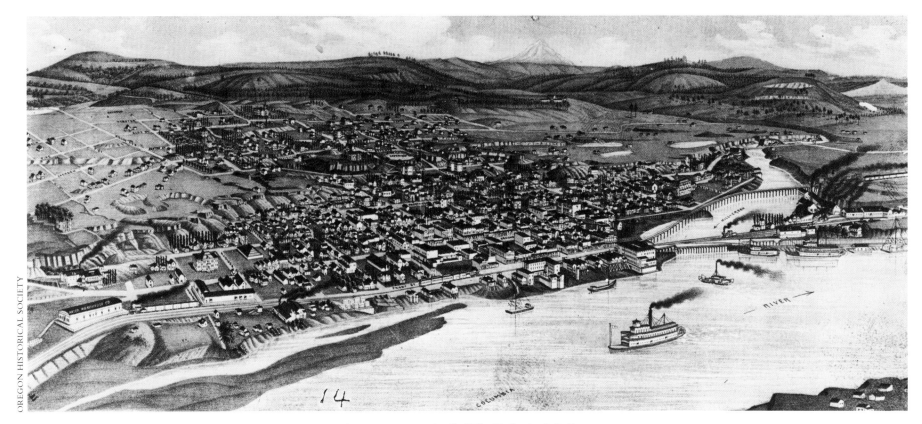

1884 "panoramic view" of The Dalles by J. J. Stoner.

favorably, a style of architecture having been adopted, entirely unsuited to a Military post on the frontier, and the arrangements of the buildings such that if assigned as proposed every officer would have more, I believe, than double his authorized number of rooms, and the finishing throughout, with interior and exterior being of the most elaborate and costly character, notwithstanding the high price of labor and materials. The quarters built for and occupied by Col. Wright, a double house with two full stories and attic, [are] such as I have never seen occupied by a private gentleman except at or in the neighborhood of our large Eastern cities; certainly no private residence at all comparable to it can be found on the Pacific.

The bitter attacks on Fort Dalles' architecture led to cuts in funds, but Jordan's detailed defenses of his actions — and his warnings about security threats — staved off drastic action, including his dismissal. Many officers were demanding his head. Among the cuts made were Jordan's continual requests for fire fighting equipment. Jordan improvised a water line from hollowed-out cottonwood trunks, but it wasn't enough; fires eventually destroyed most of his wood structures. The "good taste" and fame of Jordan's buildings helped lead to their demise.

Jordan finally returned to the East in the winter of 1860-61, but Fort Dalles stayed in business serving immigrants until 1867, when it was finally abandoned and absorbed by the growing town. An 1891 fire leveled 20 blocks; today only one building, the restored Surgeon's Quarters, still remains — a reminder of the town's "picturesque" origins.

A gold rush began in 1861 in eastern Oregon, Idaho and British Columbia, and The Dalles became even more of a booming supply center—as well as a victim of rampant inflation. A shortage of workers led to high wages, but the cost of living also leaped. The number of saloons jumped to 25. The federal government built a mint at The Dalles because so much gold came through town, but the mines fizzled out before any coins were ever minted. General James Rusling, noting The Dalles' decline after the mining boom ended, wrote that the "town of some two thousand inhabitants was already in its decrepitude" and "now at a standstill, if not something worse; her few merchants sat by their doors watching for customers in vain." Nonetheless, General Rusling credited The Dalles "with a maturer civilization than any we had seen since leaving Salt Lake." The fort had initially provided a steady market for beef and grain, especially wheat, and these enterprises continued to grow steadily. The Dalles-Boise military road was built in 1869, and three years later construction began on The Dalles-Sandy wagon road, now known as the Old Pioneer Road.

The Dalles–Celilo portage, 1867, by C. E. Watkins.

Paths were being cleared through the wilderness, but steamboats continued to dominate travel on the Columbia and in the Gorge—and were often the only means of communication—until 1883, when the first railroad was completed through the Gorge. The whistle that signalled the arrival of a steamboat at one of the Gorge's many landings was an exciting event, but today the once well-known names of the docks have been nearly forgotten; Butler, Breslin and Mt. Pleasant Landings were near my family's home.

Even the fancy new sternwheelers couldn't ascend the falls and rapids of the Gorge, however, so control of steamboat travel on the Columbia depended upon control of the portages at the Great Cascades and The Dalles/Celilo Falls. The Oregon Steam Navigation Company (OSN) was formed by a group of consolidating rivals headed by a steamboat captain, John Ainsworth. A combination of floods and business acumen gave the OSN, by the mid-1860s, a monopoly on Columbia River traffic.

The north bank Cascades portage by C. E. Watkins.

The Regulator *and Castle (Beacon) Rock. 1899 Gifford photo.*

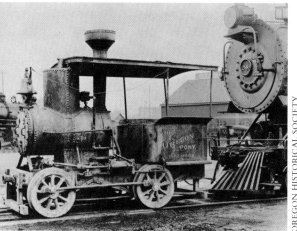

The Oregon Pony.

The company soon made high profits from the increased river traffic due to army shipments and gold strikes in Idaho. While playing the portage owners at the Great Cascades against each other, Capt. Ainsworth brought the first locomotive, the *Oregon Pony,* to the Northwest. It began service on the Eagle Creek-Cascade Locks run in 1862 and covered passengers transferring between steamboats with soot.

Puget Sound business interests hated the OSN because it brought settlers and commerce to Portland instead of Seattle; in 1864, the Washington legislature passed a bill authorizing the condemnation of the OSN's lands on the north bank of the Great Cascades and the construction of a new portage railroad to compete with the "unscrupulous monopoly." The OSN usually defeated potential competitors with rate wars, but this time the OSN had to persuade the U.S. Congress to override the state of Washington's actions.

The Tahoma *trapped in ice near Archer Mountain, 1916.*

Steamboats (and later, trains) were a boon to commerce, but only served the main route through the Gorge. People journeying to communities away from the river had to walk or rent horses and wagons from livery stables. Teunis Wyers, beginning with three Cayuse ponies, established a stage line which for decades delivered passengers and mail from White Salmon to Trout Lake and Camas Prairie (now called Glenwood). His stage coaches, which traveled about four miles-per-hour, were usually pulled by four-horse teams, but some stretches, such as Bingen to White Salmon, required more horsepower. Another stage line ran from Rockland (Dallesport) to Goldendale via Columbus (Maryhill); it replaced Pony Short, the horseback mail carrier. Ferryboats began service at important crossings, such as the Cascades, Hood River, Underwood, The Dalles and Grant (near Rufus); some of these ferries remained in service until the 1950s.

Klickitat Landing (Lyle) by Gifford.

The New Western Queen *ferry (ca. 1917) at The Dalles, where ferries ran until a toll bridge was built in 1954.*

Ben Snipes and others built cattle empires around Camas Prairie; after the roundups, the cattle were driven to the Columbia, usually at Klickitat Landing (Lyle), and loaded onto steamboats for shipment to markets. Sheepmen began ferrying their large herds of "hoofed locusts" (as John Muir labeled them) across the Columbia and summering them on Mt. Adams' lush meadows; one Oregon firm moved 10,000 sheep to Mt. Adams each summer. The local cattlemen fought back, including with vigilante raids; most of the "Indian scares" in Klickitat County after 1856 were actually cattlemen trying to frighten off sheepherders and other potential newcomers. Cattlemen at Camas Prairie wanted federal regulation of sheep grazing and were instrumental in the establishment of Columbia Forest Reserve, now Gifford Pinchot National Forest.

The citizens of Klickitat County, trying to avoid taxes, fought the state's efforts to force them to establish a county government; and the

Whiskey Row in Stevenson two years after the disastrous 1914 fire.

Beacon Rock and the Icehouse fishwheel at low water.

OSN monopoly brought all of its "floating property" to Klickitat County at tax time in order to avoid Oregon taxes. The cattlemen failed to keep newcomers out; enough people settled at John J. Golden's new town to move the county seat, in a bitter 1878 election, to Goldendale from Rockland, the cattlemen's choice—and the scene of considerable land fraud involving Rev. O.D. Taylor and others.

Downriver in Skamania County, the county seat was moved from Lower Cascades (North Bonneville) to Stevenson—in the middle of the night! Irate commissioners, angered by a rent increase, secretly took the county records upriver to one of George Stevenson's buildings. The resulting controversy was settled by the great flood of 1894, which swept over the rickety ex-courthouse at Lower Cascades; the historic documents would have been lost had they not been "stolen." A visitor to the Upper Cascades area in the 1890s wrote that it was "inhabited by Hon. George H. Stevenson and about one million mosquitos. Mr. Stevenson runs two fish wheels and represents Skamania County in the lower house of the legislature. The mosquitos run everything else."

This resort on the Wind River recently reopened. Many luxurious hot springs resorts were built in Skamania County about the turn-of-the-century.

This 900-pound female sturgeon was caught at The Dalles in 1951; it was 82 years old and 11 ½ feet long.

Icehouse Wheel and Beacon Rock.

Fishwheels were uniquely suited to the Columbia Gorge. Small versions were in use on North Carolina rivers as early as 1829, but were not introduced on the Columbia until 1879, when Sam Wilson built one at the Cascades. British writer Rudyard Kipling visited the Columbia a decade later, when dozens of fishwheels were operating, and described them as an "infernal arrangement of wire-gauze compartments worked by the current to scoop up the salmon as he races up the river." Since they were powered by the river's current, the large, rotating scoops were very efficient — if they were located at the right spot. Fishwheels cost thousands of dollars each to build, so they were a gamble; but the catch could be as much as 68,000 pounds of salmon a day. William McCord's first fishwheel collapsed from the weight of the salmon that overfilled its scoops. Giant sturgeons sometimes got stuck in the fishwheels; they were usually killed and thrown back into the river.

Frank Warren, who later died when the *Titanic* sunk, built a cannery at Warrendale to reap the bounty and leased Bradford Island, my ancestors' burial site, for 99 years in order to build fishwheels there; other canneries opened at Dodson and Rooster Rock. Salmon caught in fishwheels at the lower Cascades were floated down the river to the canneries, where they were hauled in by boats; about one thousand pounds of fish, strung together with rope, were attached to each float (an empty cask).

Fishwheels mounted on scows could fluctuate with the river levels.
C. E. Watkins photo taken at the Williams wheel site near Bradford Island.

Rooster Rock Cannery was moved downstream because of silting.

Indian shelter and a fishwheel near Celilo Falls.

The Dalles-Celilo stretch of the river was the other favored site for fishwheels. River channels at Celilo were enlarged with dynamite to increase the catch of fishwheels, and snipers with .44s were stationed to shoot seals, since they scared away the salmon—and ate too many. The Seufert Brothers Co. was the major operator of fishwheels around The Dalles; its cannery east of town packed the salmon for nation-wide distribution (as well as fruit from the brothers' irrigated orchards). Seufert Brothers also fished with seines; the loaded nets often had to be hauled with horses. 35 tons of salmon were once caught in a single day in a Seufert seine operation below Celilo.

Local Indians operated some of the fishwheels at The Dalles and Celilo, but their prosperity was limited by the potlatch tradition, which encouraged a redistribution of wealth to those less fortunate. Sam Williams, the bishop of the Shaker Church east of The Dalles, owned some scow wheels—which helped to support many of his congregation. Bishop Williams even threw an annual Thanksgiving dinner for non-Indian hobos; this feast was usually held in the cottonwoods along the banks of the Columbia below the town of Hood River.

25 tons of salmon in Warren's cannery.
1903 Kiser Bros. photo.

Kalliah and her younger daughter, Abbie Estabrook.

My great-grandfather, Johnny Stooquin, and two of my distant relatives, Frank Estabrook and Johnny Baughman, helped construct William Sams' fishwheels at the lower Cascades. My great-grandmother, Kalliah Tumalth, best known as "Indian Mary," was a strong and liberated woman, proud of her heritage. She was still a baby when her father was hung, and she grew up during the worst time of all for Native Americans in the West. When grown, she moved back downriver to Skamania, where she was awarded a contract by the federal government to meet the steamboats at Marr's Landing and deliver the local mail by horse.

Kalliah's first husband was Henry Will-wy-ity (or Will-wy-i-tit), a Wish-ham Indian who died in 1872. After his death, she took another husband, Johnny Stooquin, a Wish-ham jockey. But he eventually returned to the Yakima Reservation, and Kalliah spent quite a bit of time with Lou Marr, a white neighbor who lived with his brother, Kenzy, near Franz Lake. Lou Marr spoke the Cascade Indian dialect, and one evening a week they would speak only her native language so that she wouldn't forget it. (Their friendship led to family gossip about another paleface in the woodpile.) Lou Marr was murdered during a robbery; his killer was hanged. Kalliah later married Louis Gerand, part French, part Cowlitz Indian, and the father of her youngest daughter, Abbie.

Even though the Cascade Indians never ceded that part of so-called Skamania County within the Columbia Gorge to the federal government, Kalliah had to trade a team of horses to homesteaders to buy 160 acres at Skamania. Some unscrupulous local Whites realized that as an Indian, Kalliah could not legally own land; they tried to lay claim to her property. In an unheard-of action, evidently because of her government mail contract, the U.S. Land Office in Vancouver wrote a letter threatening the claim jumpers and convinced Congress to pass a special bill to hold the land in trust for her. Most of her original land is still jointly held by her descendants.

Kalliah lived in a cabin—later moved by the railroad—on a low ridge overlooking the Columbia's scenic but swampy floodplain. Almost a century later, her orchard is still producing apples, pears, quinces and grapes. The second half of the 19th century was an extremely racist period in U.S. history, but Kalliah fortunately enjoyed the respect of most of her white neighbors. The mail delivery contract allowed her to meet white newcomers on a friendly basis and provided a "respectable" lifestyle. She also had a considerable knowledge of medicine and often

At Kalliah's cabin: Carrie, Pearl and Nina (my father's older sisters); Kalliah/Mary; and my Uncle Ray. A nearby creek and road are named for Indian Mary, but all traces of her cabin have disappeared into the berry vines.

recommended that sick neighbors visit the hot springs near North Bonneville, the same now-commercial springs my father bathed in as a child. Some of her white neighbors liked Kalliah so much that they occasionally affectionately called her "White Mary," a "compliment" she — of course — despised.

Kalliah died in 1906; my grandmother was already married at the time, but she and my grandfather, a "squaw man," were living with "Indian Mary." The view from Kalliah's cabin site is still much the same as it was when she lived there, but the radical changes in the landscape a few miles upriver at her birthplace, the Great Cascades, had already begun before her passing.

This somewhat bizarre photo (plains-style clothes, painted backdrop, etc.) is probably of Johnny Stooquin.

133

COPYRIGHT 1902 BY
BENJ. A. GIFFORD
THE DALLES ORE. 234 NORTH ABUTMENT TO BRIDGE OF THE GODS, AND CASCADES OF THE COLUMBIA.

*This Gifford photo of the Cascades and an inoperative fishwheel shows the
source of the slide material that created the rapids.*

The Charles R. Spencer *beats the* Bailey Gatzert *to the Cascade Locks, 1908. Races between the steamboats were common, evidently to the amusement of the passengers. The part of the government locks not submerged by the Bonneville reservoir can still be seen in the park at Cascade Locks, the mill town once known as Whiskey Flats for its abundance of saloons. Sawyer photo.*

In 1878 the U.S. Congress authorized the construction of a canal and locks to bypass the Great Cascades of the Columbia, making the portage unnecessary. However, it was almost two decades before The Dalles became a seaport.

Bad weather and shortages of materials and federal funds prevented the opening of the locks until 1896. By then the river travel had already begun to decline because of competition from the railroads. The U.S. Army Corps of Engineers was guilty of outrageous cost overruns even then; originally estimated at only $700,000, the locks eventually cost $3,820,629 to build. An eight mile long canal bypassing the Narrows and Celilo Falls was finally completed in 1915; by then river travel had nearly vanished, not to enjoy a resurgence until the reappearance of the Corps of Engineers decades later.

The Oregonian *published a special edition in 1896 to celebrate (finally!) the opening of the locks.*

135

8. *Where in the Sam Hill?*

Crown Point.

I do not know much about gods; but I think that the river
Is a strong brown god—sullen, untamed and intractable,
Patient to some degree, at first recognized as a frontier;
Useful, untrustworthy, as a conveyor of commerce;
Then only a problem confronting the builder of bridges.
The problem once solved, the brown god is almost forgotten
By the dwellers in cities—ever, however, implacable,
Keeping his seasons and rages, destroyer, reminder
Of what men chose to forget.

—T. S. ELIOT

The Dalles during the great flood of 1894.

How soon the Columbia River was forgotten by the fickle settlers! The once-essential boats were needed less and less; they were soon superseded by trains and automobiles. The Gorge's importance as a transportation corridor, however, didn't diminish.

Cape Horn from Breslin Landing. C. E. Watkins photo.

137

PILLARS OF HERCULES

Henry Villard was a German immigrant who became a prominent American journalist. He came to the Northwest to investigate the Oregon and California Railroad for a group of German investors who had purchased many of manager Ben Holladay's inflated floating bonds. Villard ended up not only gaining control of the O & C and Willamette Valley transportation systems, but also purchasing the Oregon Steam Navigation Company. He consolidated these companies in a monopoly, the Oregon Railway and Navigation Company (OR&N).

Villard began acquiring land along the south bank of the Columbia in 1879 for his transcontinental railroad; local service to the Gorge began the following year. The OR&N line from Portland to Minnesota was completed in 1883; it finally linked the Northwest to the eastern states and is now called the Union Pacific.

Ten years later Canadian James J. Hill completed a transcontinental railroad, the Great Northern, from Minnesota to Seattle, finally fulfilling Governor Stevens' dream. In 1908 Jim Hill built his S.P.&S. Railroad through the Columbia Gorge along the north bank; it is now the Burlington Northern that roars by my cabin.

Cliffs (once Chamberlain Flats), the town on the north bank where the John Day Dam was later built, became a bustling railroad town. But when the S.P.&S. moved its switching yard downriver to Fallbridge (which the railroad rechristened Wishram over the objections of local residents), Cliffs became a ghost town. One entrepreneur quickly moved into the deserted Columbia Hotel and, using the grand hotel's stationery and credit rating, ordered and received large shipments of food, furniture and other goods before he was found out. Hobos then moved into the building; below the Columbia Hotel's sign, they hung their own sign—*Hotel de Jungle.* All "guests" were required to sign the register and ring up their room and board on the cash register that had been left behind. Horse thieves and stock rustlers took over the livery barn, so Klickitat County finally foreclosed and took over the town.

Competition was so intense between the railroad barons that tracks were laid up both banks of the Deschutes River for many miles before the companies finally came to their senses. Chinese "coolies" were brought to the Northwest in large numbers to build the railroads. Many stayed, including a large community in The Dalles, and later did most of the work in the salmon canneries. They, too, were victims of violent attacks by white racists, who claimed that the Chinese stole their jobs by working for cheaper wages.

The OR&N's track through the Pillars of Hercules was a favorite of train photographers.

Logging increased in the Northwest when steamboats and gold rushes combined to provide practical markets. After the railroads were built and the eastern forests depleted, logging the giant, virgin evergreens became the region's major industry. Simon Benson, the "boss logger of all Oregon," bundled and towed logs to his San Diego mill.

Logs were brought down to the river and railroads by oxen (on skid roads), in flumes and later by incline railroads. Logs from Larch Mountain were floated down a flume to the mill at Bridal Veil; Broughton Lumber Company's flume, still in operation, can be seen on the cliff above Drano Lake (named for "French Billy" Drano). The engines of the steep incline railroads were called "steam donkeys" and started many forest fires. A load of logs on the steep track up Hamilton Creek once caught fire; it was released to roll down into the river to be extinguished. Instead, the fire spread along the entire length of the track and burned most of the watershed. Clearcuts and fires, especially the infamous 1902 Yacolt Burn, quickly denuded the slopes above Skamania and elsewhere.

Living conditions were generally poor in logging camps, and the loggers — letting off steam after working long, hard hours — were notoriously rowdy. Clifton Hughes, an early Skamania County resident, wrote about logging after the "steam donkeys" replaced oxen:

We then had donkey skinners and donkey punchers, whistle punks, hook-tenders, hookers, chasers, choker setters, high-climbers, the swing and yarders, roaders, bull-blocks, cawk-shoes and tin pants, gandy-dancers and hog-heads and an important person the bull-cook, who carried in the split wood to the cook shack, carried the drinking water and swept out the bunk house and many other chores, and told far fetched tales.

My father's father for a while drove a wagon that supplied logging camps on the Washougal River, where logging practices were exceptionally destructive. Log dams were built in steps up the river, and the resulting ponds were filled with logs. The dams were then dynamited, one after another, and the logs swept down to Parker's Landing at Washougal. This practice ended when the scheme backfired one year; a huge log jam formed that blocked further operations.

Flume to the Bridal Veil mill.

My grandpa and his tote team at Breslin's Warehouse, Cape Horn, about 1892.

My paternal grandfather, also Charles Williams (although he went by "Charley"), was born in Wisconsin the week after President Lincoln's assassination in 1865. After his father returned from the Civil War, the family moved to Pipestone, Minnesota, the site of the famous quarry where the red stone used for Indian "peace pipes" comes from. My grandpa ran away from home because he couldn't get along with his stepmother and stepbrother; among other jobs, the young boy drove horse-drawn streetcars in Omaha, Nebraska, and repaired combines.

He migrated to Tacoma by railroad ("by the cars," as it was called) in 1889, the same year Washington became a state. After working as a carpenter in Tacoma, he moved to the Columbia Gorge. At first he drove a tote team, which supplied a logging camp; then he worked on a fishing scow, catching salmon and sturgeon. When he was 30, he met and married my beautiful Cascade grandmother, Amanda; the newly-weds moved into the cabin with her mother, Kalliah, where the first two of their eleven children were born. My grandparents farmed at Cape Horn for a while, but returned to "the old place" at Skamania.

My grandma was an enrolled member of the Yakima Confederated Tribes, as were many of the Cascade Indians. Once the family moved, by horse and wagon, to her allotment near Wapato on the Yakima Reservation, where they farmed for a couple of years before returning home to the Gorge. My favorite story about my grandmother took place at the Wapato farm. [32]

When cattle accidently eat too much alfalfa, they get gas bubbles that can be fatal. The usual cure was to puncture the cows' sides, but my grandmother was totally opposed to this, claiming that the animals never fully recovered. Once when her husband was away, their cows got into an alfalfa field and were dangerously sick. My grandma refused to puncture them; instead, she spent all night getting the cows' rear ends propped up higher than their heads on bales of hay so the gas could escape. She saved all of the cows.

My grandparents, Amanda and Charley Williams, with my older aunts and uncle at the Cape Horn farm, 1902.

Another of my favorite stories about my Indian grandma involves my Aunt Faye, who, with a friend, had gotten into some mischief and were being chased by a man with a whip. The young girls made it back to my grandma who calmly looked up at the man and softly said: "I guess you'll have to whip me first." Saved!

About the time World War I started, my grandparents moved to "downtown" Skamania and lived on the ledge where the Grange Hall now stands. They later moved down the hill into the Sams' general merchandise store, where my father, their youngest child, was born; my cabin is near where the barn stood. They ran the store and post office until 1928, when my grandpa took a job lathing houses in Washougal. They moved back to Skamania in 1932, and my grandpa worked during the depression as foreman of a WPA mosquito-control project. He and the other men backpacked sprayers and cans of oil to kill the mosquito larvae in the Gorge's numerous ponds.

My grandpa and a denuded Skamania County landscape; the name of his larger horse was Heather Jack.

"Downtown" Skamania, with the general store/post office and the Grange Hall, in 1914.

The Vista House on Crown Point.

Most of the Oregon parks along the Scenic Highway were gifts of Portland's rich, but Shepherds Dell (above) was donated by George Shepherd, a local citizen of modest means. Cross & Dimmitt photo.

My other grandfather, Frank Deffenbaugh, came from Nebraska and worked on the construction of the old highway on the Oregon side of the Gorge. Parts of it still remain as the Columbia River Scenic Highway. This old highway was a labor of love, and the passage of time, especially the thick growth of moss, has only increased its appeal.

A drive to build a highway into the Gorge began in 1909, but interest waned after a few short sections were completed. An influential and wealthy Seattle lawyer, Samuel Hill, was obsessed with road building and revived the effort. He admonished Portland's civic leaders to "cash in, year after year, on our crop of scenic beauty."

On one of his many trips to Europe, Hill was accompanied by Samuel Lancaster. Hill took the young highway engineer to the famous Axenstrasse highway in Switzerland, and near Bingen-on-the-Rhine in

Germany, Hill showed him dry masonry walls (stone walls without mortar) that dated from Charlemagne's time—and suggested that Lancaster design a road into the Columbia Gorge using similar construction. By 1913 the Columbia River Highway was authorized; Lancaster was hired as the chief engineer.

Wahkeena Falls.

Sam Lancaster became paralyzed from the neck down as an adolescent; he was able to walk again only through painful, hard work. Every tendon had to be broken loose, moved back into place and then exercised and massaged until it could function. Drawing with a pencil held in his teeth, Lancaster designed a frame with rollers to help his recovery (and later furnished similar devices to disabled children). The miraculous recovery made him a religious man, and he decided to devote his life to helping society and instilling a love of nature in other people.

Lancaster was overwhelmed when he first saw the Columbia Gorge. He wrote:

The mind can only wonder at this mighty work of God, done in His own way, on a scale so great that man's best efforts appear but as the work of pigmies — the Panama Canal, a toy for children.

Lancaster thoroughly explored the Gorge route, sometimes lowering himself over cliffs with ropes. While waist-deep in ferns one day, he remembered his mother's warning: "Oh, Samuel, do be careful of my Boston fern!" He resolved that not one fern or tree would be unnecessarily damaged by his road construction, and he helped preserve the national forest lands in the Gorge "for the free use of all, in which tired men and women with their little children may enjoy the wild beauty of nature's art gallery, and recreate themselves."

Lancaster needed someone to handle the complicated logistics of building the road, so John B. Yeon volunteered to serve as roadmaster without pay. In less than two years, almost 200 miles of the highway were completed, connecting Astoria with Eagle Creek. Mushroom-shaped "half tunnels" were used to minimize cuts, and the nation's longest three-hinged arch bridge was built over Moffett Creek. At

Mitchell Point, they constructed viaducts and a tunnel with five windows (later destroyed by the progress of U.S. 30 and I–84). Craftsman from Europe were brought over to help build the dry masonry sections; according to Lancaster: "The Italian laborers built their very souls into these walls as they sang their native songs and thought of their homeland." Timber baron Simon Benson gave $10,000 to Oregon to be used in conjunction with prison labor to build the section of road across the steep slopes of Shellrock Mountain.

In 1916 the road became the first paved highway in the Northwest; President Woodrow Wilson pushed a button in Washington, D.C., that unfurled a flag over Crown Point, officially dedicating the highway and marking the beginning of the construction of Vista House, a memorial to the pioneers. Chanticleer Inn, Crown Point Chalet, Falls Chalet (near Latourell Falls) and the Columbia Gorge Hotel were erected to serve the booming tourist trade after the highway became famous through movie shorts and articles in *National Geographic* and *Scientific American.*

OREGON HISTORICAL SOCIETY

The once-famous Mitchell Point tunnel.

The menu of the Columbia Gorge Hotel.

Columbia Gorge Hotel

By some accounts, the old expression of confusion, "Where in the Sam Hill?" is derived from the dizzying hairpin turns in roads Hill built in Klickitat County. Hill, born in North Carolina in 1857, made a fortune during the railroad boom and eventually married the daughter of James J. Hill, the railroad baron. While Sam Hill's public life was exciting, his family life was a disaster. His wife spent most of her time in Washington, D.C., plus his son was disdainful of him, and his beloved daughter, Mary, was mentally unstable.

While daydreaming in his office one day, Sam Hill speculated that there must be a special place where the rain of the western slope of the Cascade Mountains meets the desert sunshine, so he sent an employee to search for this mythical agricultural Eden. The scout returned with bunches of giant grapes from the eastern end of the Columbia Gorge, and Sam Hill formed a land company in 1907 to purchase all the "ideal" agricultural land—a strip 15 miles wide and 100 miles long.

Dry masonry walls. Don Lowe photo.

Sam Hill.

146

Near Maryhill.

Near Maryhill.

Maryhill Museum.

As awesome as Sam Hill's achievements were, they never quite approached his fantasies. He did buy a considerable amount of the eastern Gorge, about 7000 acres, and began building a town for his pet project, a Quaker agricultural colony to be called "The Promised Land." But his Quaker recruits didn't share his enthusiasm for the windy, desolate area; the colony never materialized. Local people claimed that although Hill was trying to divide his land into 1200 separate tracts, they never heard anything about a Quaker colony. His new town, Maryhill, was built on the ledge above Columbus, an agricultural town founded in 1859 by Amos Stark. When much of Maryhill was destroyed by fire, Hill preserved the name by using his influence to change the name of Columbus to Maryhill.

Hill decided that his Gorge mansion at Maryhill should become a museum. He was evidently talked into this project by a close friend, the famous dancer Loie Fuller. *La Loie* claimed that she was born in a bar in Chicago and was once a child temperance lecturer. While an unknown actress in Europe, she created a captivating dance with swirling draperies and colored lights. Her dancing was rejected by the Paris Opera, but became the hit of the Folies Bergere. Sam Hill wrote to her in 1917:

After the eloquent pleading of today, I have decided to dedicate my new chateau at Maryhill, Washington, to a museum for the public good and for the betterment of French art in the Far Northwest of America. Your hopes and ideals shall be fulfilled, my dear little artist woman.

Hill convinced Queen Marie of Romania, who was grateful for U.S. aid after World War I, to dedicate his museum and to donate valuable exhibits. Gossip at the time speculated that Hill was in love with the Queen and expected her to eventually move into the mansion with him. Ignoring a scornful press, the Queen — the granddaughter of both Queen Victoria and the Czar of Russia — traveled to the Columbia Gorge in November, 1926, and dedicated the Maryhill Museum of Fine Arts to peace and beauty. Queen Marie's daughter, Princess Ileana, called Maryhill "the wildest and most desolate spot" she had ever seen.

But the museum didn't actually open for another fourteen years, when Alma de Bretteville Spreckles, widow of the sugar magnate, decided to finally fulfill her old friend's dream. Maryhill is today a fascinating, if somewhat bizarre, museum reflecting Sam Hill's diverse interests. Despite its isolation, visitors flock to see the museum's large collections of Rodin sculptures, Indian artifacts, Galle glass, dolls, icons and antique chess sets — plus a room of Romanian royal furniture.

Just east of the museum, overlooking the arid end of the Columbia Gorge, is a concrete replica of Stonehenge built by Sam Hill as a memorial to Klickitat County soldiers who died in World War I. Hill died in 1931; the Stonehenge fountain, once the center of town, and a few ruins are all that are left of his community.

Stonehenge.

149

The Sam Hill Bridge and Columbus/Maryhill from Stonehenge during the eclipse.

Eye protectors came in many styles. Craig Collins photo.

When Sam Hill built Maryhill, the Columbia it overlooked was still a wild river. Just downstream was Celilo Falls, where the remaining local Indians still fished for salmon as their ancestors had for centuries. But plans were already on the drawing board for a project that would soon doom the river, the salmon — and a way of life. The view from Stonehenge now includes — in addition to Mt. Hood and the lovely farm community of new Maryhill — the John Day Dam and its symbiotic aluminum plant. Chief Joseph's prophecy that the white people "would change the rivers if they did not suit them" has come to pass.

Druids at work. Craig Collins photo.

"Diamond ring."

Clouds parting for the eclipse.

A total solar eclipse occurred over the Columbia Gorge on February 26, 1979, and a large crowd gathered at the concrete Stonehenge replica. As happened over Stonehenge and the Gorge during the total eclipse in 1918, the rain stopped and the clouds parted for the duration of the awesome spectacle.

Total eclipse.

Reflection of the eclipsed sun on the Columbia.

9. Darkness to Dawn

Celilo Falls, 1899.

celilo fisherman

you made your nets
and tested the knots
*   seeing that they held*
little did you know
*   what was to hold you*
*   after the sound of*
*   water falling*
*   over what*
*   used to be.*

—ED EDMO 33

Where there once was a river, there is now a chain of reservoirs. The Columbia River's steep drop and its tremendous volume of water make it the nation's largest generator of hydroelectric power. The Columbia and its tributaries have now been dammed 192 times; the salmon have been traded in for "cheap" electricity, following the route of my Indian ancestors. It all began in the Gorge with Bonneville Dam during the depression of the 1930s. Now Lewiston, Idaho, is a seaport, but few salmon remain to fight their way upstream.

*Celilo Falls today – dynamited and covered by the backwaters of
The Dalles Dam. Across the river is the railroad town of Wishram.*

153

"Gill Netters near Rooster Rock," an 1891 watercolor by Cleveland Rockwell.

Little thought was given to environmental or cultural consequences when Bonneville Dam was built. The United States was in the depths of a depression, and President Franklin D. Roosevelt and almost everyone saw it as a great opportunity to put the unemployed — including my father, then just graduating from high school — to work. The dam would provide electricity for the "growth" of the wild Northwest and would finally bury the Great Cascades of the Columbia that were such an obstruction to river travel. Even Woody Guthrie, whose populist credentials seem impeccable, helped the government promote dams on the River of the West.[34] In *Roll On, Columbia,* the folksinger wrote of "turning the darkness to dawn," and his *Talking Columbia* shows how much times have changed:

> *You jes' watch this river 'n pretty soon*
> *E-ev'rybody's gonna be changin' their tune . . .*
> *The big Grand Coulee 'n the Bonneville Dam'll*
> *Build a thousand factories f'r Uncle Sam . . .*
> *'N ev'rybody else in the world.*
> *Makin' ev'rything from sewin' machines*
> *To a-tomic bedrooms, 'n plastic . . .*
> *E-ev'rything's gonna be made outa plastic.*
> *Uncle Sam needs wool, Uncle Sam needs wheat,*
> *Uncle Sam needs houses 'n stuff to eat,*
> *Uncle Sam needs water 'n power dams,*
> *Uncle Sam needs people 'n the . . .*
> > *people need land.*
> *Donat like dictators none much myself,*
> *What I think is the whole world oughta*
> > *be run by*
> *Ee-lectricity. . . .*

The salmon runs were already in decline before they were destroyed by the dams. Bad mining and logging practices had silted spawning grounds; fewer and fewer tributaries ran year-round. Early irrigation projects on the Yakima and upper Snake Rivers reduced stream flows, and overfishing took its toll.

Studies estimate that natives had been catching 18 million pounds of salmon a year from the Columbia, only about a third of what could have been caught without a decline in the runs. As to the quality, Cleveland Rockwell wrote in *Harper's Magazine* in 1882 that "salmon packed on the Columbia commands a higher price than any other."

With the advent of new technology — gill-nets and fishwheels — the catch jumped to 42 million pounds in 1883; then the decline began. The catches did not decrease much until after the turn of the century, primarily because (as now happens with whales) the less-desirable species were increasingly exploited as the favored ones disappeared. Even though fishwheels took only a small portion of the total catch, fierce competition between gill-netters and fishwheel operators resulted in traps and fishwheels being outlawed by the time dam construction began in earnest.

Grand Coulee Dam was built far upriver on the Columbia at the same time that Bonneville Dam transformed the Gorge. When the gates of the Grand Coulee Dam were closed, 1100 miles of spawning grounds were wiped out. Columbia salmon spawned as far inland as Nevada until the Owyhee Dam was built in 1934. Irrigation dams blocked runs on the Snake and Deschutes Rivers, both famous for fishing.

In the 1950s, it was The Dalles' turn for the Corps of Engineers' boom-and-bust economics. The Dalles Locks and Dam were authorized in 1950, and construction on the long powerhouse began two

Salmon can label ca. 1900 (Seufert Collection).

The Dalles Dam and the Shaker village.

years later. With the construction boom, the ferry at The Dalles was finally replaced by a bridge. The Dalles Dam was completed in 1957, flooding Celilo Falls, and Congress authorized the John Day Dam at the east end of the Gorge to complete the steps of dams up to the mouth of the Snake River.[35] An interstate highway, I-80N (now I-84), was built through the Gorge; and the series of locks that accompanied the dams brought back river travel, much of it barges filled with wheat.

Now developers of the Gorge had water, rail and freeway transportation to offer potential industries. The main problem seemed to be getting rid of the huge surplus of electricity generated by the new dams. Enter the aluminum industry, one of the most polluting and energy-intensive of all. With huge federal subsidies, aluminum plants were built at Troutdale, The Dalles and below the beautiful cliffs at the John Day Dam; another was almost built near Bonneville Dam, as was a steel plant. The aluminum industry now uses *one third* of the power produced by the Columbia's dams, and utilities are building coal and nuclear plants along the Columbia River.[36]

Water projects, such as the $6 million The Dalles Irrigation Project begun in 1961, have opened the arid lands along the upper Columbia to intensive agriculture; irrigation now accounts for over 85% of the water

taken from the Columbia. Pesticide runoff and poor agricultural practices along streams have also hurt fish populations. Now leaking radioactive wastes at the Hanford Works Atomic Reservation have given the Columbia a reputation of being "the most radioactive river in the world."

Despite the Columbia's many fish hatcheries, the river catch is now down to almost nothing; Columbia River salmon species may soon be declared endangered. The spawning salmon are unable to pass many of the dams, and fishladders have been only partially successful. According to a six-year study by the U.S. National Marine Fisheries Service, 20-30% of the fingerling salmon are killed by *each* dam, with a cumulative death rate of 75-95%. The Corps of Engineers' "Operation Fish Run" is now attempting to truck and barge the young fish around the dams, with mixed results.[37]

The disappearance of the salmon has led to bitter, even violent battles between Indian and white fishermen. Many white fishermen — commercial and sport — claim that Indians should not receive such "special privileges" as fish quotas. The tribes reply that they *reserved* these fishing rights when they signed the treaties that ceded their lands; federal courts have agreed. The annual runs are now so scanty that the conflict is almost academic, and Indian and white river fishermen are finally joining forces to limit the ocean catch of the salmon before they enter the rivers.

When Celilo Falls, the last major fishing site in the Gorge, was covered by the Dalles Dam, the members of the treaty tribes were given monetary compensation — after a bitter fight — and assigned other fishing sites between The Dalles and Bonneville Dams. But an era and a way of life died when Celilo Falls disappeared, and such things are beyond compensation. Across the freeway from the site of the former falls is the Celilo Village, which, in the tradition of the area, is administered jointly by the Warm Springs, Yakima and Umatilla Tribes.

The Corps of Engineers' latest project, a few miles upriver from my cabin, is the $575 million (minimum) construction of a second powerhouse at Bonneville Dam; the Corps calls it: "Building Tomorrow Today." A small town, North Bonneville, was moved so that a huge pit could be dug. After the new dam/powerhouse is built in the hole, a river channel will be excavated so that the Columbia will also flow through this new powerhouse. Kidney Lake, a favorite swimming hole, was filled by the Corps for no apparent reason.

Ice on the Columbia near Dog Creek Falls, winter of 1978-9.

The Corps has brought boat travel back to the Gorge. Mt. Hood and Hood River in the background.

Even though I had sympathy for the residents being moved, there was poetic justice in moving the town of North Bonneville for the second powerhouse project; it was built on top of my ancestors' village to house construction workers for the original Bonneville Dam. Another shack town, "Bonnevilla," rose across the river, below the mouth of Tanner Creek. The Corps of Engineers treated the North Bonneville residents so shabbily that the town has turned the tables on the Corps. There is now a large new town, bankrolled by the federal taxpayers, sprawled over what was prime wildlife habitat. Hamilton Island no longer exists. Speculation has fueled many controversies, and the new town is many times larger than the original. Now the town wants the Corps to buy more flood plain for future expansion and to provide annual funds for maintaining the new parks and other facilities. When the Corps finishes the second powerhouse in 1982, it plans to move across the river and relocate the town of (South) Bonneville in order to build new locks because the ones at Bonneville are narrower than the others on the Columbia.

After Tumalth, my great-great-grandfather, was hanged, he was laid to rest on Bradford Island. When Bonneville Dam was built, the island became the connector between the dam's two sections; Tumalth had to move again. His remains and those of his neighbors on the island were rudely placed in a common grave in the Old Pioneer Cemetery where Kalliah and other of my ancestors are buried. Now the second powerhouse project has brought the neglected cemetery a new neighbor, a concrete plant. The tiny cemetery's old-growth firs are now a serene anomaly amidst an unnatural act.

Whenever I have to pass the new powerhouse site, that huge pit illuminated with floodlights at night, writer Joseph Wood Krutch's comment usually comes to mind:

> *When man despoils a work of man,*
> *we call him a vandal.*
> *When man despoils a work of nature,*
> *we call him a developer.*

Bradford Island during the original Bonneville Dam construction.

OREGON HISTORICAL SOCIETY

Tumalth's village site today.

10. Reclamation

Some of my friends who talk glibly of the right of any individual to do anything he wants with any of his property take the point of view that it is not the concern of federal or state or local government to interfere with what they miscall "the liberty of the individual." With them I do not agree and never have agreed, because, unlike them, I am thinking of the future of the United States. My conception of liberty does not permit an individual citizen or group of citizens to commit acts of depredation against nature in such a way as to harm their neighbors.

—President Franklin D. Roosevelt at
the Dedication of Bonneville Dam, 1937

Conservation efforts began early in the Columbia Gorge, but have never been able to keep up with the development that has resulted from the Gorge's role as a major transportation corridor and power generator. Protection has come in cycles; civic pride, especially in Portland, has resulted in periodic campaigns to "save the Gorge." Each time, a few threatened areas are usually rescued from development before interest wanes or a war intervenes. The Gorge now faces unprecedented threats, and the controversy raging over its future is one of the country's major conservation battles.

Multnomah Falls before the foot bridge was built.

Benson State Park.

Trains once brought visitors to Multnomah Falls. Prentiss photo.

Near Lost Lake.

Oregon National Forest, renamed Mt. Hood, was established in 1908. When construction of the Scenic Highway in 1915 spurred interest in preserving the Gorge, the U.S. Forest Service established its first campground and, with the help of Portland's business elite, protected 14,000 acres between Warrendale and Viento. Trails were begun up Eagle and Herman Creeks, and the system was later greatly expanded by the Civilian Conservation Corps (CCC). Lumber baron Simon Benson bought Multnomah Falls for $5000 and donated the area for a park; other gifts led to many state parks on the Oregon side.

John Yeon headed the first Columbia Gorge Commission, which in the 1930s, during the initial dam construction, fought efforts to turn the Gorge into the "Pittsburgh of the West." In the 1950s, Gertrude Jensen, with the help of the Portland Women's Forum, saved more crucial areas. The struggle over Beacon Rock, however, probably best symbolizes environmental battles in the Columbia Gorge.

Rooster Rock State Park.

Little Beacon Rock. Much of Beacon Rock State Park was recently opened to off-road vehicles (without public hearings).

Beacon Rock is a basalt plug towering more than 800 feet above the river, the remnant core of a volcano that pushed its way a few million years ago up through the older layers of earth that have since worn away; the base covers seventeen acres. The Cascade Indians called it *Che-che-op-tin.* Lewis and Clark originally referred to it as "Beaten Rock" in their diary, but on their return trip corrected this to Beacon Rock, notating "the head of tide water." It became Castle Rock for a while, but the name was officially changed back in 1916.

The first ascent to the top was made in 1901, and the climbers found foxglove and many other flowers in bloom atop the monolith. The climb was a major event, as evidenced by the coverage in *The Oregonian:*

The start was made from the base at 7 in the morning and by 11:30 Smith, Purser, and Church, the latter a 17 year old boy, who acquitted himself with great credit, were plainly visible from below and were given a great demonstration. Their shouts and revolver shots were heard all over the countryside. Farmers rushed out to fire their shotguns. Women waved their aprons. The first salute to them was from a freight train that whizzed by on the OR&N. The engineer tooted his whistle repeatedly.

Because of its proximity to the Columbia and the railroad, Beacon Rock had long been coveted by exploiters. In 1915 Henry Biddle bought Beacon Rock to save it from quarrying; then he commenced to fulfill his

dream: a trail to the top. When blasting began for the trail, an elderly Cascade Indian man warned Biddle that the gods would retaliate. According to Biddle, "a succession of violent sleet and snow storms" ensued. More than two years and $10,000 later, Biddle and his foreman, Charley "Tin Can" Johnson, a veteran of the Scenic Highway project, finally finished the 52-switchback trail to the top, where the vista is one of the best there is of the Gorge.

When the U.S. Army Corps of Engineers began to construct jetties at the mouth of the Columbia River in 1931, Beacon Rock was again deemed a logical source of rock. Biddle's heirs tried to donate Beacon Rock and the nearby waterfalls to the state of Washington for a park, but the governor refused, claiming that the owners' generosity really amounted to a form of tax evasion. Disturbed by this turn of events, Sam Boardman, on behalf of the Oregon State Parks, appealed to J. C. Ainsworth, the influential president of the U.S. National Bank:

I am enclosing a news item pertaining to the destruction of Beacon Rock; also a letter from the Vancouver Chamber of Commerce. I believe that this historical landmark should have the protection of a sovereign state. Governor Hartley of Washington has refused to accept it. Oregon can ill afford to leave it to the whims of commercialism. If in your wisdom, will you intercede with the heirs of Henry Biddle and with Mr. Erskine Wood?

Should we not lift our hands to preserve one of the scenic marvels of the Columbia River? The river is a boundary line but it does not obscure our vision. Should it stifle our scenic preservation?

The owners agreed to deed Beacon Rock and the Pool of the Winds Falls to the state of Oregon for the sum of one dollar, and Boardman began a spirited defense of the gift:

Why should we let the width of a river destroy a scenic asset woven into a recreational garland belonging to both states? How can we stand by and see the death of a relative, though a bit distant? If such things as beauty were not fought to a safe conclusion, the waters of Multnomah Falls would be falling through steel pipes for the generation of electricity.

Washington newspapers were outraged; one writer protested that Oregon was "overstepping her recreational boundaries." Embarrassed Washington citizens, including the Granges and even the Stevenson Chamber of Commerce, convinced incoming-Governor Martin to reverse the previous governor's stand; Beacon Rock became a Washington State Park.

From atop Beacon Rock. The Corps of Engineers plans to dump dredge spoils on these islands—and a promoter wants to dock an ocean liner at one of the islands and convert it into vacation condominiums.

Oregon has thirteen state parks in the Gorge downstream from Bonneville Dam; Washington has one: Beacon Rock. But the management of the Oregon parks could be much better. The state parks are supervised by the Oregon Highway Department, and little wilderness surrounds the expensive showcase campgrounds. (And out-of-state campers are charged an extra fee — to the annoyance of Washingtonians.)

However, the management of the state parks and national forest lands is the least of the Gorge's problems. Wildlife populations are rapidly declining, and the Gorge's famous vistas, such as from Crown Point, will soon be degraded. The *Willamette Week* warned its readers:

Marvel at this scenery today, for it may be radically altered tomorrow. The new I-205 bridge and expanding Vancouver electronic plants promise to propel the present residential sprawl in Clark County eastward into rural Skamania County, which has no zoning law. Apart from an ordinance that requires a minimum two-acre-lot size for septic tank and well purposes, and a few other minor restrictions, developers have carte blanche to tear up the rolling farmlands between Washougal and White Salmon.

The Port of Hood River wants to build a causeway over to Wells Island and then subsidize the island's industrial development, at the expense of its heron rookeries. The plan is now on appeal before the Land Conservation and Development Commission.

Thanks to state Sen. Ken Jernstedt, the Port of Hood River also has been awarded $300,000 from the state's revolving port fund for the creation of an inland "industrial park," a plan bitterly opposed by many orchardists who fear the eventual conversion of the Hood River valley into an industrial complex.

The Washington Department of Natural Resources wants to clear-cut Table Mountain, across from Cascade Locks. Private timberland in the Bridal Veil Falls area between Rooster Rock and Multnomah Falls is already being clear-cut, as is much of Hood River County's timberland in the gorge. And gravel mining near the Columbia east of Hood River continues to eat away the cliffs along the old scenic highway.

No single government authority exists to stop, or even slow down, the rape of the gorge—Oregon's, and perhaps the nation's, most spectacular unprotected scenic wonder. Over 50 federal, state, county and local government agencies share decisions about the gorge; most of the power rests with county commissioners, port districts and energy officials. So far, most successful thwarting of potentially harmful developments in the gorge has been by private legal action and organized by citizen pressure.

Rooster Rock State Park includes a nude beach and huge parking lots.

Since the above photo was taken, this pond in Rooster Rock State Park was partially filled with dredge spoils; cattle were allowed to graze in the park on what had been one of the Gorge's largest surviving wappato patches.

Even though it is a major transportation corridor, the Columbia Gorge is still a scenic wonder: a spectacular mixture of rugged wilderness, pastoral farmlands and historic towns. This delicate balance, however, is now severely threatened by heavy industrialization, suburban sprawl, mining of the escarpments, destructive logging practices and even more dams.

Skamania County official graffito.
Vera Dafoe photo.

East Bingen. Vera Dafoe photo.

Skamania County across the river from Crown Point, a national landmark, does not even have zoning regulations.

From Dallesport.

The port authorities, with sweeping powers and few restraints (or ports, for that matter), are responsible for many of the Gorge's controversial developments. The ports had been relatively harmless until the Economic Development Administration (EDA) started awarding them millions of dollars in federal revenue-sharing funds. New flood-control dams far upstream are also aiding industrialization along the floodplain; there are plans to industrialize even some of the islands.

Two of the most immediately threatened areas are the floodplains that form the western entrance to the Gorge: the delta of the Sandy River on the Oregon side, and Steigerwald Lake, the former camas and wappato marshes just east of Washougal. The latter, a pastoral gateway to the Gorge, is now used for agriculture but has been rezoned for heavy industry by Clark County and is being rapidly covered with mobile homes and industrial parks.

The further industrialization planned by the Port of Camas-Washougal for the Steigerwald Lake wetlands would threaten the endangered Columbian white-tailed deer, the bald eagle, the red fox and the river otter. This port authority has already killed the salmon runs on Gibbons Creek by not honoring its promise to provide fish passage around its dikes; the bald eagles that once fed on these salmon have been reduced to dining on carp. The port directors claim that their leapfrog industrialization is needed to provide jobs for young people; in response, three-fourths of Washougal's high school students signed a petition opposing further destruction of the wetlands. The port authority, with the help of Congressman Mike McCormack, recently tried to industrialize more wetlands in violation of environmental laws, but local conservationists threatened to sue and blocked the $1.3 million in federal funds earmarked for the project (a top priority of Governor Dixie Lee Ray). The port authority also obtained a permit in 1979 from the Corps of Engineers to build a barge terminal at Cottonwood Beach, a popular wild shoreline near Washougal, even though it already owns an unused barge terminal nearby.

The Port of Klickitat County is using federal funds to court industries to build plants at Dallesport, now farms and beautiful sand dunes; 6000 acres on the peninsula have been rezoned for industry. A zirconium plant similar to Albany, Oregon's, Wah Chang plant (a notorious polluter) was almost built at Dallesport in 1978; when local citizens insisted on pollution controls, the company, Western Zirconium, decided to move the plant and its cat-box smell to Utah. Across the river at The

The Gorge's islands, such as this one near Rowena, provide priceless wildlife habitat.

Sand dunes near Skamania Landing subdivision.

plats approved early in the century to build large numbers of houses around Crown Point and Dodson.

Probably the most insidious threat to the Columbia Gorge is the boom in residential building. The new interstate bridge (I-205) to be completed in 1982 will make the most critically threatened stretch of the Gorge — Washougal to Beacon Rock — a bedroom community of Portland. Skamania County still does not even have zoning regulations, in spite of strong local support for them. Local residents of Klickitat County have sued the county over subdivisions of dubious legality on the spectacular bluffs east of Bingen; similar suits are pending in Skamania County.

The non-profit Nature Conservancy has purchased part of Rowena Plateau, famous for spring wildflowers, but nearby Rowena Dell, a unique oak canyon, is being subdivided. The famed Hood River Valley orchards nestled beneath Mt. Hood are threatened by industrial parks, resorts and condominium complexes (especially Mt. Hood Meadows) despite the opposition of a majority of the local residents. The town of The Dalles is trying to annex two hundred acres of fruit orchards for its urban growth.

Dalles, the owners of the aluminum plant, one of the Gorge's main employers — and polluters, lost suits brought by cherry growers for damage to their orchards.

The Port of Cascade Locks tried to build a tourist tramway up the Gorge's escarpment to Forest Service lands being considered for Wilderness designation, but local conservationists went to court and again blocked the federal subsidies it would require. This port authority, through pressure on the Hood River County commissioners, has blocked the Forest Service's planned purchase of scenic lands at Wyeth, across from Wind Mountain. The port, claiming that the town of Cascade Locks has no more room for growth, is promoting large housing developments at Wyeth, but a recent survey showed that there were enough housing sites within the town's growth boundary to accommodate *quadruple* the existing population. The Trust for Public Lands, a non-profit organization, purchased over 500 acres at Wyeth, preventing development until county approval is obtained for Forest Service purchase. As at Wyeth, developers are trying to use subdivision

Rowena Dell is being subdivided.

The spectacular cliffs east of White Salmon are being mined and are threatened by subdivisions of dubious legality.

The mouth of Duncan Creek — after a flood washed out Skamania Landing's recreational dam, which had blocked steelhead runs for a decade.

Two of the worst forms of visual blight in the Gorge are clearcuts and mines. The slopes above Skamania and Stevenson, visible across the river from the most visited part of the Gorge, have already been badly scarred by rampant road-building and huge new clearcuts.[38] Mining, including gravel pits on islands, is booming, virtually unregulated. The beautiful areas just east of Hood River and Bingen are being devastated by quarries, including a stretch along the old hand-built highway, which could be a fine bicycle path. Woodward Creek near Beacon Rock was recently illegally quarried. The area around Bridal Veil Falls is being both mined and clearcut. The worst offender among the public agencies on both counts is Washington's Department of Natural Resources (DNR), which claims that it legally must fully exploit *all* of its lands. High on DNR's list for clearcutting are Table Mountain and the slope near Greenleaf Falls.

Many small tributaries in the Gorge have been damaged by gravel mining and clearcutting: they are polluted with herbicides and logging slash and silt, and fewer and fewer run year round. Fresh water mussels were once numerous in Duncan Creek, the stream I live near and drink from, but they have disappeared; an early pioneer wrote that his uncle "caught 300 trout in one day in Duncan Creek." Steelhead were also once plentiful in Duncan Creek — until the Skamania Landing sub-dividers dammed it at the mouth for a swimming hole and, despite earlier promises, would not open the dam for the winter runs.

Claiming a "moral obligation to develop" the White Salmon River, the Klickitat County Public Utility District (PUD) is planning to build seven dams and five powerhouses between Trout Lake and the Columbia. The PUD's consultants attempted to overcome environmental objections by offering to dye the concrete dams and powerhouses green. The White Salmon's only dam was built in 1913; it blocked the spawning of the "salmon" the river was named for. Local conservationists, farmers, wildlife agencies and the Yakima Tribal Council have filed petitions to intervene in the licensing of the proposed dams, but so far have not been able to obtain federal support for their alternative: remove the unneeded Condit Dam and restore the once-important fishery. They feel that fishery enhancement is the type of project that should be funded by the Mid-Columbia Economic Development District, the agency that provides the ports with their federal subsidies.[39]

Now Skamania and Clark County PUDs are studying the Little

Ice on Duncan Creek.

175

Mouth of the Klickitat River.

White Salmon River for power generation, and there was yet another campaign recently to dam the free-flowing Klickitat River, one of the best remaining fisheries. Moreover, the U.S. Army Corps of Engineers and the Bonneville Power Administration (BPA) plan to use the Columbia's dams for peak power loads; this practice will cause the water levels in the reservoirs to fluctuate many more feet daily than they now do, further devastating salmon and other wildlife — and leaving a bathtub ring along the river. Many Gorge residents, pointing to the damage caused by The Dalles, John Day and Bonneville Dams, feel that the Columbia Gorge has already made enough sacrifices for energy dues.

The situation in the Gorge was summed up in the March/April 1980 issue of *Pacific Northwest:*

Both cooperation and dissension across state and county lines are boiling around the Columbia River Gorge. As reported in the December issue, the gorge area is subject to many demands, including more dams, clearcuts, and gravel quarries, by both private interests and state agencies. The local residents, trying to keep the scenic value and rural life of the gorge intact, are calling in federal help to encourage the formation of a National Scenic Area under the National Park Service.

The gorge is truly one of the world's natural wonders —and to the Northwest, perhaps the most intriguing spot geologically as well as historically. This conspicuous stretch of river —with its small but effective group of resident activists, The Columbia Gorge Coalition, will certainly gain some degree of special protection, perhaps in time to rescue it from predictably short-sighted concepts of river management.

Even though much natural landscape still remains, local conservationists feel that the varied assaults are now so overwhelming that development in the Columbia Gorge is approaching a critical point. Most agree that immediate federal action is necessary because the many agencies with jurisdiction in the Gorge will never agree on a way to save the Gorge (and since the Gorge is undeniably of national significance, the federal government should be involved in helping to relieve local taxpayers of the financial burden of preserving it). Like Lake Tahoe to the south, the Gorge is split between two states that seldom agree on anything. Bi-state agreements have failed miserably at Tahoe, and Governor Jerry Brown of California now believes that the only alternative left is the establishment of a national recreation or scenic area. Big Sur and Jackson Hole are also being considered as prototype national scenic areas.

Mouth of the Deschutes River. Many of the Gorge's tributaries should be protected as wild and scenic rivers.

Oregon and Washington each have a Columbia Gorge Commission, but the commissions have neither powers nor funds; they must rely on the cooperation of the many counties involved, and the results range from occasionally encouraging to frequently dismal. A typical example is Hood River County's recent granting of a permit to again quarry Government Cove — despite the strong opposition of both Gorge commissions. At a stormy meeting early in 1980, the Oregon Gorge Commission refused to endorse (as ordered) Governor Vic Atiyeh's

Government Cove east of Cascade Locks.

letter to Interior Secretary Cecil Andrus, which claimed that the Gorge was already adequately protected and opposed federal help. So Atiyeh, at the urging of the port authorities, removed the deciding vote (a popular conservationist) from the commission. [40]

Local conservationists, with the help of regional and national environmental groups, have formed the Columbia Gorge Coalition, a "non-profit organization of concerned citizens dedicated to preserving the Gorge's scenery, recreation, agriculture, and heritage." The Hood River-based coalition wants Congress to establish a Columbia Gorge National Scenic Area; its brochure describes the innovative concept: [41]

A National Scenic Area is a new approach to scenic preservation—a parkland with a minimum of public acquisition. The Columbia Gorge could have been a superlative national park, the equal of Mt. Rainier, Crater Lake or Yosemite, but is already too developed to make such protection practical. The proposed National Scenic Area, like Japanese and European national parks, would let appropriate uses continue under mixed public and private ownership. Critical lands and recreation would be protected, as would farms and fisheries.

A joint local-state-federal commission would formulate, with public participation, a unified management plan for the Gorge. The commission would identify key areas and appropriate protective measures to ensure the objectives of the scenic area. Zoning, purchase of easements, and tax incentives would be emphasized, so cost would be minimal, compared with traditional parks.

A National Park Service managed core area in the west end of the Gorge would provide for outdoor recreation; much of this area is already in public ownership.

The National Scenic Area should extend from the Sandy River and Washougal at least to the Maryhill Museum and Stonehenge. A shorter area would exclude the most important archeological sites and the desert portion of the Gorge's remarkable biotic spectrum.

The north-south boundary would generally be rim-to-rim, but should include the spectacular tributary valleys such as the White Salmon, Klickitat and Hood Rivers. Their valuable fisheries and farmlands would be subject to accelerated development pressures if not included in the Scenic Area.

A primary goal of the National Scenic Area would be to protect agricultural lands from conversion to subdivisions and industrial plants. Financial incentives would be available to help farmers, orchardists, and ranchers maintain their lands that contribute so much to the Gorge's economy and scenic beauty.

Hunting and fishing would continue under present jurisdictions and treaty rights. An important goal of the Scenic Area would be to protect and rehabilitate wildlife habitat and fisheries.

The site of Condit Dam (as construction started) on the White Salmon River, which was an incredible fishery—until the low output dam was built.

Mt. Hood from near White Salmon.

The Columbia Gorge Coalition elaborates further on the benefits of the proposed parkland to local residents:

People enjoy living in the Gorge because of its exceptional beauty and rural character. These qualities would be preserved by the National Scenic Area, and the locally-based tourist and agricultural economies would be enhanced.

Future development would occur within the growth boundaries of existing towns, which could continue to provide more jobs by attracting clean industry.

Since the emphasis would be on protecting lands while continuing private ownership, the tax base would be maintained and residents would not be forced off their property. Some lands would be acquired for recreation or wildlife habitat, but on a willing-seller basis. Speculative taxes would be removed from rural property.

Portland and Vancouver residents are fortunate to have a recreational area as spectacular as the Gorge so nearby, and the value of protecting the Gorge will increase with future gas shortages. Large reserves managed by the National Park Service have been established near many cities in the last decade, but thus far the Northwest has been ignored (even though its Congressional delegation holds key committee positions and could easily win approval for a Gorge park).42

The National Park Service released a comprehensive study of the Columbia Gorge in the spring of 1980. The controversial report confirmed conservationists' charges that the Gorge's wildlife and rural character were rapidly disappearing; it details four alternatives for the Gorge's future: status quo, strengthening the existing Columbia River Gorge Commissions, management by a joint federal-state-local commission, and a national recreation area. (The Columbia Gorge Coalition's recommendation is a combination of the latter two.)

Now the administration will make a formal recommendation to Congress. Conservationists are hopeful, especially since Assistant Interior Secretary Bob Herbst advocates "areas of national concern," public-private partnerships similar to the proposed Columbia Gorge National Scenic Area. The fate of the Gorge probably rests with the U.S. Congress, especially since Governors Victor Atiyeh and Dixy Lee Ray, unlike their predecessors, oppose federal help and more protection for the Gorge.

John Yeon, the noted architect and coauthor of the first environmental study of the Gorge, calls the Columbia Gorge "the noblest unprotected landscape in the United States." In a letter to Governor Atiyeh, Yeon traced the history of efforts to preserve the Gorge, noting that "voluntary interstate cooperation has been advocated for 40 years and has brought us only to the present peril." He continued:

It must be assumed that all of the forces which are threatening the Gorge will raise shrill objections to its preservation. Already you can hear them. Even local government agencies with no profiteering ambitions may react negatively towards a greater public good if they sense encroachment on their present turf; the old territorial reflex. And there will always be those who would sacrifice the Gorge on their ideological altar of free enterprise. I am a free enterpriser myself, but I don't believe that free enterprise can fight international wars or save large-scale interstate landscapes.

A Columbia Gorge National Scenic Area would be an important milestone in the history of the national park idea; it would set a precedent for protecting scenic natural and agricultural lands of national significance that are no longer wild enough to meet the traditional criteria for national parks. Local conservationists stress that immediate action is needed before the Columbia Gorge is further degraded so as to be unfit for even the new flexible park concepts; they fear that the Gorge is rapidly approaching its critical mass—the point of no return.

Reclamation of a new kind is needed—and fast!

1871 etching of Beacon Rock.

From atop Beacon Rock.

Beacon Rock about 1900. George Weister photo.

Edward Curtis photo of a Wishham woman and the Narrows.

I guess I am a dreamer, too, though not as ritualistic as my forebears have been. I dream about the day, not too far off, when I and the other residents of the Columbia Gorge who worship the beauty and history surrounding us can again relax and not be tormented by daily assaults on our home.

Sometimes, sitting atop Beacon Rock during a full moon, I even dream about a future time, one with a more benevolent technology, when I can see, hear and feel the power of the Great Cascades, the Long Narrows and Celilo Falls; important parts of our stolen heritage. Dreamers haven't fared well in the Columbia Gorge—but this time it's up to you.

Where there is no dream, the people perish.

— PROVERBS 29:18

East toward Bonneville Dam from atop Beacon Rock. Since this photo was taken, much of the vista has been covered by North Bonneville—and the new town wants the rest of the floodplain for expansion and industrialization.

Fairy Falls.

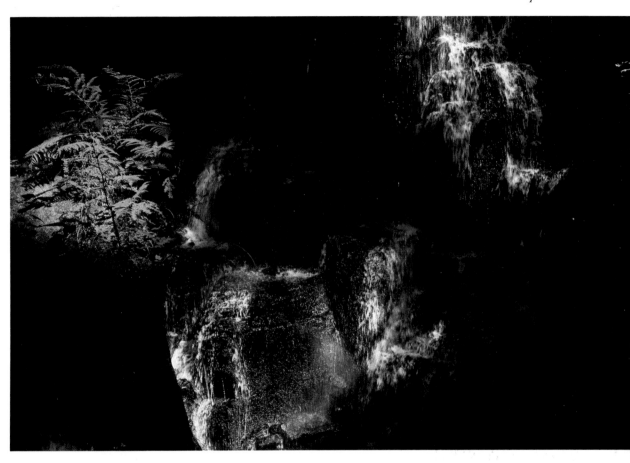

It is imperative to maintain portions of the wilderness untouched, so that a tree will rot where it falls, a waterfall will pour its curves without generating electricity, a trumpeter swan may float on uncontaminated water —and moderns may at least see what their ancestors knew in their nerves and blood.

— Bernard DeVoto 43

These wild places are where we began. When they end, so do we. We had better not speed their passing ... These places don't need to go. They do not have to be an arena in which man carries on his old habits and makes his old mistakes until the naturalness of a place is demolished or even demeaned. Man's genius, if he really has one, can surely find ways to go back over the bruised places, heal them, and let them sustain his civilization.

—DAVID BROWER

Friends of my grandparents at the Rooster Rock cannery; Crown Point in the background.

Horsetail Falls.

"View of the Dalles on the Columbia River" from an early government report.

. . . and so there ain't nothing more to write about, and I am rotten glad of it, because if I'd knowed what a trouble it was to make a book I wouldn't a tackled it and I ain't agoing to no more. But I reckon I got to light out for the Territory ahead of the rest, because Aunt Sally she's going to adopt me and sivilize me and I can't stand it. I been there before.

—MARK TWAIN

Footnotes

1. Sigurd Olson is a noted writer and conservationist from the Boundary Waters area of northern Minnesota.
2. N. Scott Momaday is a Kiowa Indian and a literature professor; his first novel, *House Made of Dawn,* won a Pulitzer Prize.
3. John Burroughs was an influential naturalist and writer in the early days of the environmental movement.
4. There are numerous versions of the Bridge of the Gods legend—and many are of dubious authenticity. The version I give came primarily from my grandmother (and a book she gave me, *Legends of the Klickitats*) and incorporates Coyote stories that were normally told separately. There were even legends about a Chief Big Foot, whose feet were three feet long.
5. Five was considered a magic number by most prehistoric residents of the lower Columbia.
6. John Muir was a famous naturalist and writer; he cofounded the Sierra Club and is considered the father of Yosemite National Park.
7. The Eagle Creek Formation sits atop the Gorge's oldest exposed formation, a layer of Oligocene basalt flows and breccias called the Ohanapecosh Formation (or Skamania Volcanics), outcrops of which are visible on the north bank near Washougal.
8. The lower levels of the Troutdale Formation along the Gorge's western edge are often referred to separately as Sandy River Mudstone.
9. The east wall of Hood River Valley is a 2000 foot high fault escarpment.
10. The *Atlas of Oregon Indians* warns that "the relevant question in comparing technologies, for example, is not whether the dugout canoe was as fast as an outboard motorboat, but whether the canoe served the needs of the people who used it." (Gas shortages were not a worry.)
11. Shahala means "above," the name used by the Chinooks at the river's mouth. Wahlála means "small lake," for a lake at Upper Cascades. The Cascades possibly called themselves the Katlagakya (middle people). The name *Chinook* is confusing as it refers to a language, a cultural group and a village/tribe on the north bank at the mouth of the Columbia.
12. *Chuck,* in Jargon, means water or river, and the Great Cascades were called *Hi-yu Shookum Chuck:* "very strong waters." Many of the "Indian" words I use in this book are Jargon.
13. An aspect of lower Columbian village life that appalled the white settlers was waste disposal. Trash, such as fish bones, was dumped in mounds near the villages—fortunately for archeologists. The reek of the dumps, combined with that of the drying fish, shocked the pioneers; but the lack of European-style sanitation evidently wasn't much of a health problem until the exotic diseases arrived. (The "smell of money" is relative.)
14. Another demigod, Blue Jay, the "zany actor," was the power spirit of going over the edge, insanity. The mere mention of his name would usually make Chinooks laugh, though nervously.
15. Waterfalls were often called *tum-tum,* the sound of a heart beating.
16. Some accounts claim that Kalliah's sister, Virginia Miller, was the last person laid to rest on Memaloose Island, but she was actually buried in the Old Pioneer (and Indian!) Cemetery near North Bonneville.
17. The Spedis Owl form was named for the Spedis family, well-known residents of Spearfish (near the Wishram village site). Spearfish became the major off-reservation Upper Chinook settlement when commercial fishing brought many of them back to the river.
18. Sahaptin (a dialect of Sahaptian) and Chinookan are both Penuitan languages.
19. Since tribes used each others' territories for seasonal food gathering, the "cooperative food site sharing" encouraged peaceful relations among neighboring tribes.
20. The first person I heard use "illegal alien" in this manner was Charlie Hill, a Seneca comedian, on a Richard Pryor TV show.
21. Since Indians did not have written languages, the spelling of their names varied considerably. There are many versions of Tumalth's name, including Tomalt, Tomalsh and (via Edward Curtis) Támañl.
22. The Feather Religion and a similar religion, Washat, are still popular on the Yakima Reservation. For more on the "revivalistic" religions, see James Mooney's *The Ghost Dance Religion: Smohalla and His Doctrine,* Cora DuBois' *The Feather Cult of the Middle Columbia* and H. G. Barnett's *Indian Shakers.*

23. "Breed" and "blood" are still used derogatorily by some Indians to describe people that are part-White, part-Indian. Fortunately, "siwash," the White's derisive term for Indians in the Northwest, is rarely heard anymore. Siwash began as the Jargon word for an Indian, but had become the equivalent of "nigger" by the time my father was a boy.

24. Sam Barlow's toll road was so steep that wagons had to be winched up or down parts of it. Trees were often cut down and dragged behind wagons to slow them down, resulting in huge piles of trees at the bottom of hills.

25. Some accounts claim that Narcissa Whitman was lacing melons with a substance to nauseate thieves of them (Indian or wolf, depending upon the version) and thus gave further credence to the poison conspiracy theory.

26. For more on Saule, see Lucile McDonald's *Coast Country*.

27. Some villages near the confluence of the Deschutes River and the Columbia even offered to return "borrowed" immigrant property as a goodwill gesture. Some Klickitats, meanwhile, began forays into their old territory south of the Columbia. They raided Willamette Valley settlements, but later helped settlers capture Rogue Indians that were also raiding Whites.

28. Joel Palmer blamed the extensive thefts at Ft. Gilliam on "jews."

29. The confusion of claims later led to considerable litigation between the federal government, Methodists, Catholics and the city of The Dalles.

30. One soldier called Peu-peu-mox-mox's scalp "a beauty, the hair about eighteen inches long, all braided in with beads and eagle feathers." Peu-peu-mox-mox's name meant Yellow Bird or Yellow Serpent.

31. One paper claimed that three Klickitat chiefs were unjustly arrested, then escaped and led the attack on the Joslyns' house. Joslyn sued the U.S. Government for the damage done to his home; the litigation dragged on for the rest of his life.

32. The government's allotment program took reservation lands held in common by the tribes and divided it into parcels owned by individual tribal members. In addition to bringing the concept of private property to the Native Americans, it opened the "excess" lands (after allotments were made) to white settlement and ownership. During the allotment period, the Yakima Tribe welcomed the Cascade Indians with open arms (since less land would be lost with increased tribal membership), but later tried to purge Cascades from tribal roles. Years of bitter battles resulted.

33. Ed Edmo is a Native American poet and the host of a TV program, *Indian Time*. He lived at Celilo Falls, including when the falls disappeared.

34. Guthrie worked as a "public relations consultant" for the Bonneville Power Administration (BPA) in order to promote public power — and counter the private utilities' "anti-socialism" campaign against FDR's dream of public utilities.

35. The Dalles Dam was officially dedicated in 1959 by then-Vice President Richard Nixon.

36. BPA's electricity rates were standardized throughout the region so that areas around the dam sites (especially the Gorge) would not be able to lure industries with cheaper power rates.

37. The young fish die from nitrogen bends and from being chewed up by turbine blades. The problem will probably be even worse when "peaking" — huge daily fluctuations in reservoir levels — begins. The Corps is condemning lands along the river, such as Dickey Farms at Bingen, that will be flooded and is building up other areas, such as Mayer State Park, to keep them above the fluctuating water levels.

38. In the last two decades, Skamania County officials have covered the county and Gifford Pinchot National Forest with roads paid for by its share of national forest revenues (more than $1000 per county resident annually). It's a local "joke" that the county will build a paved road to anyone's property. Before-and-after maps in Sterling's *The South Cascades* graphically show how a large wilderness disappeared in a few years. Pinchot is one of the country's worst managed national forests.

39. Some PUD officials want to build nuclear power plants in Klickitat County, but opposition is strong.

40. Atiyeh ended up signing the *Washington* Gorge Commission's letter — and whited out the embarrassing letterhead when he sent copies to other officials. Washington's Governor Ray, at a Vancouver press conference, soon repudiated her promise to Andrus of state protection of the Gorge. For more of the governors' antics in response to the National Park Service study of the Gorge, see the newspaper aticles by Alkire and Moser listed in the bibliography.

41. For further information, contact the Columbia Gorge Coalition at P.O. Box 266, Hood River, Oregon 97031. They need your help!

42. National (urban) recreation areas established recently include: Golden Gate (San Francisco), Santa Monica Mountains (Los Angeles), Gateway (New York), Chattahoochee River (Atlanta) and Cuyahoga Valley (Cleveland). Similar National Park Service areas include Point Reyes (S.F.), Cape Cod (Boston) and Fire Island (N.Y.) Nat'l Seashores, Indiana Dunes Nat'l Lakeshore (Chicago) and Biscayne Nat'l Monument (Miami). Also, national recreation areas surround many of the country's major water impoundments, but not in the Gorge. And the Columbia Plateau, which includes the east end of the Gorge, is virtually unrepresented in the National Park System.

43. Bernard DeVoto was an influential conservation and history writer and edited a concise, readable version of Lewis and Clark's journals.

Bibliography

Alkire, Tom. "Twilight for the gorge." *Willamette Week*. April 21, 1980.

Allen, John Eliot. *The Magnificent Gateway*. Forest Grove: Timber Press, 1979.

Alt, David, and Hyndman, Donald. *Roadside Geology of Oregon*. Missoula: Mountain Press Publishing Co., 1978.

American West Editors. *The Great Northwest*. Palo Alto: American West, 1973.

Anastasio, Angelo. *The Southern Plateau: An Ecological Analysis of Intergroup Relations*. Moscow: University of Idaho, 1975.

Attwell, Jim. *Columbia River Gorge History*. Skamania: Tahlkie Books, 1974 (Vol. 1) and 1975 (Vol. 2).

Attwell, Jim. *Early History of Klickitat County*. Skamania: Tahlkie Books, 1977.

Balch, Frederic Homer. *The Bridge of the Gods: a Romance of Indian Oregon*. Portland: Binfords & Mort, 1965.

Baldwin, Ewart. *Geology of Oregon*. Eugene: University of Oregon, 1964.

Ballou, Robert. *Early Klickitat Valley Days*. Portland: Metropolitan Press, 1938.

Bancroft, Hubert Howe. *The Native Races of the Pacific States of North America* (Vol. 1). New York: D. Appleton and Co., 1875.

Biddle, Henry. *Beacon Rock on the Columbia*. Portland: Lewis and Clark Trail Heritage Foundation, 1978 (reprint of 1924 article).

Boit, John. "Remarks on the Ship Columbia's Voyage from Boston on a Voyage Round the Globe." *Proceedings* Vol. LIII (June 1920).

Braasch, Gary. "The Rise and Fall of the Columbia River Gorge." *Oregon Rainbow* Vol. 1, No. 2 (Summer 1976).

Brown, Donald A. *History of the Cascades*. Unpublished manuscript, 1935.

Bullard, Oral. *Crisis On the Columbia*. Beaverton: The Touchstone Press. 1968.

Bullard, Oral, and Lowe, Don. *Short Trips and Trails, The Columbia Gorge*. Beaverton: The Touchstone Press, 1974.

Bullitt, Harriet (ed.). *Pacific Northwest* Vol. 14, No. 2 (March/April 1980).

Bundy, Don. "Gorge feels sting of political winds." *The Oregonian*. March 17, 1980.

Bunnell, Clarence. *Legends of the Klickitats*. Portland: Binfords & Mort, 1933.

Clark, Ella. *Indian Legends of the Pacific Northwest*. Berkeley: University of California Press, 1953.

Columbia River Gorge Commissions. *A Resource Management Program for the Columbia Gorge*. Stevenson: States of Oregon and Washington, 1976.

Cressman, L.S. *Prehistory of the Far West*. Salt Lake City: Univ. of Utah, 1977.

Curtis, Edward. *The North American Indian*. Norwood, Mass.: Plimpton Press, 1911 (20 volumes).

Daugherty, Richard. *The Yakima People*. Phoenix: Indian Tribal Series, 1973.

DeVoto, Bernard (ed.). *The Journals of Lewis and Clark*. Cambridge: The Riverside Press, 1953.

Donaldson, Ivan, and Cramer, Frederick. *Fishwheels of the Columbia*. Portland: Binfords & Mort, 1971.

Donaldson, Strong and Strong. *Shortcourse-on-the-Columbia*. 1974. (This 25¢ booklet, the best bargain for learning about the Gorge, includes historic maps. Available from the Skamania County Historical Society.)

Flanigan, James. "Study considers gorge for national reserve." *Oregon Journal*. March 28, 1979.

Franchère, Gabriel. *Narrative of a Voyage to the Northwest Coast of America*. New York: Redfield, 1854. (Translated & edited by J. V. Huntington; a more recent edition was edited by Hoyt Franchère.)

French, David. "Wasco-Wishram." *Perspectives in American Indian Culture Change* (Edward Spicer, ed.). Chicago: University of Chicago Press, 1961.

Glassley, Ray. *Indian Wars of the Pacific Northwest*. Portland: Binfords & Mort, 1953.

Harper, Russell. *Paul Kane's Frontier*. Austin: Univ. of Texas, 1971.

Hart, John. "Parks For The People: The National Debate." *Sierra* Vol. 64, No. 5 (Sept./Oct. 1979).

Harvey, A. G. *Douglas of the Fir*. Cambridge: Harvard Univ. Press, 1947.

Hill, Beth and Ray. *Indian Petroglyphs of the Pacific Northwest*. Seattle: Univ. of Washington Press, 1974.

History Committee. *History of Skamania County*. Stevenson: 1957.

Interstate Publishing Co. *An Illustrated History of Klickitat, Yakima and Kittitas Counties*. Evansville: Unigraphic, 1977 (reproduction of 1904 original).

Johansen, Dorothy, and Gates, Charles. *Empire of the Columbia*. New York: Harper & Row, 1957.

Jolley, Russ. *Survey of Wildflowers and Flowering Shrubs of the Columbia Gorge*. Preliminary manuscript, 1979.

Jones, Roy Franklin. *Wappato Indians*. Privately printed, 1972.

Josephy, Jr., Alvin, and Lavender, David. *The Great West*. New York: American Heritage Publishing Co., 1965.

Judson, Katharine. *Myths & Legends of the Pacific Northwest*. Chicago: A.C. McClurg & Co., 1910 (reprinted by the Shorely Book Store).

Kelley, Plympton J. (Wm. Bischoff, ed.). *We Were Not Summer Soldiers*. Tacoma:

Washington State Historical Society, 1976.

Kiser Bros. *Pacific Coast Pictures*. Portland: Wonderland Souvenir Co., 1904.

Knuth, Priscilla. *"Picturesque" Frontier: The Army's Fort Dalles*. Portland: Oregon Historical Society, 1968.

Ladiges, Jerry. *Glenwood, Formerly Camas Prairie*. Privately published, 1978.

Lancaster, Samuel. *The Columbia: America's Greatest Highway Through the Cascade Mountains to the Sea*. Portland: Privately published, 1915.

Lawrence, Donald. "The Submerged Forest of the Columbia River Gorge." *The Geographic Review* Vol. XXVI, No. 4 (Oct. 1936).

Lawrence, Donald and Elizabeth. "Bridge of the Gods Legend, Its Origin, History and Dating." *Mazama* Vol. XL, No. 13 (Dec. 1958).

Lee, W. Storrs (ed.). *Washington State: A Literary Chronicle*. New York: Funk & Wagnalls, 1969.

Lobb, Allan, and Wolfe, Art. *Indian Baskets of the Northwest Coast*. Portland: Graphic Arts Center, 1978.

Lockley, Fred. *History of the Columbia River Valley From The Dalles to the Sea*. Chicago: S. J. Clarke, 1928 (3 volumes).

Lyman, William. *The Columbia River*. Portland: Binfords & Mort, 1963.

Mills, Randall. *Stern-wheelers up Columbia*. Palo Alto: Pacific Books, 1947.

Moser, Pat. "Everyone agrees the gorge is beautiful, but..." *The Columbian*. April 13, 1980.

National Park Service. *Study of Alternatives — Columbia River Gorge*. Denver: Dept. of the Interior, 1980.

Natural Resources Defense Council. "Waste in the West (Part II)." *NRDC Newsletter* Vol. 7, No. 1 (Jan./Feb. 1978).

Neils, Selma. *So This Is Klickitat*. Klickitat: Woman's Club/Metropolitan Press, 1967.

Plotts, Lois Davis. *Maryhill, Sam Hill and Me*. Privately published, 1978.

Ramsey, Guy Reed. *Postmarked Washington*. Goldendale: Klickitat County Historical Society, 1977.

Ramsey, Jarold (ed.). *Coyote Was Going There: Indian Literature of the Oregon Country*. Seattle: University of Washington Press, 1977.

Ray, Verne. *Cultural Relations in the Plateau of Northwestern America*. Los Angeles: The Southwest Museum, 1939.

Ross, Alexander. *Adventures of the First Settlers on the Oregon or Columbia River*. London: Smith, Elder and Co., 1849.

Ruby, Robert, and Brown, John. *The Chinook Indians: Traders of the Lower Columbia River*. Norman: University of Oklahoma Press, 1976.

Seaman, N.G. *Indian Relics of the Pacific Northwest*. Portland: Binfords & Mort, 1967.

Secretary of War. *Explorations for a Route for a Pacific Railroad*. Washington, D.C.: U.S. Government, 1860.

Skamania County Historical Society. *Skamania County Heritage* Vol. 5, No. 1 (June 1976) and Vol. 7, No. 1 (June 1978).

Spier, Leslie, and Sapir, Edward. *Wishram Ethnography*. Seattle: University of Washington, 1930.

Stallard, Bruce. *Archeology In Washington*. Seattle: The Shorely Book Store, 1967 (reproduction of Information Circular No. 30 originally published by the state of Washington).

Stenzel, Franz. *Cleveland Rockwell, Scientist and Artist, 1837-1907*. Portland: Oregon Historical Society, 1972.

Sterling, E.M. *The South Cascades: The Gifford Pinchot National Forest*. Seattle: The Mountaineers, 1975.

Strong, Emory. *Stone Age on the Columbia River*. Portland: Binfords & Mort, 1959. (Emory Strong also edited *Wakemap Mound and Nearby Sites on the Long Narrows of the Columbia River*.)

Suchanek, Ron. "The Columbia River Gorge: The Story of the River and the Rocks." *ORE BIN* Vol. 36, No. 12 (Dec. 1974).

Swanton, John. *Indian Tribes of North America* (Bureau of American Ethnology Bulletin No. 145). Washington, D.C.: Government Printing Office, 1952.

Thomas, Nancy. "The Columbia Gorge: A National Treasure." *Pacific Search* Vol. 13, No. 12 (Dec./Jan. 1979-80).

Thwaites, Reuben Gold (ed.). *Original Journals of the Lewis and Clark Expedition, 1804-1806*. New York: Antiquarian Press, 1959 (8 volumes).

Timmen, Fritz. *Blow For the Landing*. Caldwell: Caxton Printers, 1973.

Townsend, John. *Narrative of a Journey Across the Rocky Mountains to the Columbia River*. Philadelphia: Henry Perkins, 1839.

Underhill, Ruth. *Indians of the Pacific Northwest*. Washington, D.C.: Dept. of the Interior (B.I.A.), 1945.

Vaughan, Thomas. *Paul Kane: The Columbia Wanderer*. Portland: Oregon Historical Society, 1971.

Warren, Esther. *The Columbia Gorge Story*. Privately published, 1977.

Washington Pioneer Project. *Told by the Pioneers*. Olympia: Work Projects Administration, 1938 (3 volumes).

Watkins, C.E. *Photographs of the Columbia River and Oregon*. Carmel: Friends of Photography, 1979.

Weeks, James. *One Part of the West*. The Dalles: Original County Courthouse, 1978.

Williams, Ira. "The Columbia River Gorge: Its Geologic History." *The Mineral Resources of Oregon* (Oregon Bureau of Mines and Geology) Vol. 2, No. 3 (Nov. 1916).

Williams, Marsha. *First White Descriptions of the Shahala (Cascade) Indians*. College paper, 1971.

Wilson, Fred, and Stewart, Earle. *Steamboat Days On the Rivers*. Portland: Oregon Historical Society, 1969.

Zucker, Jeff (ed.). *Atlas of Oregon Indians*. Manuscript in preparation.

From Crown Point.

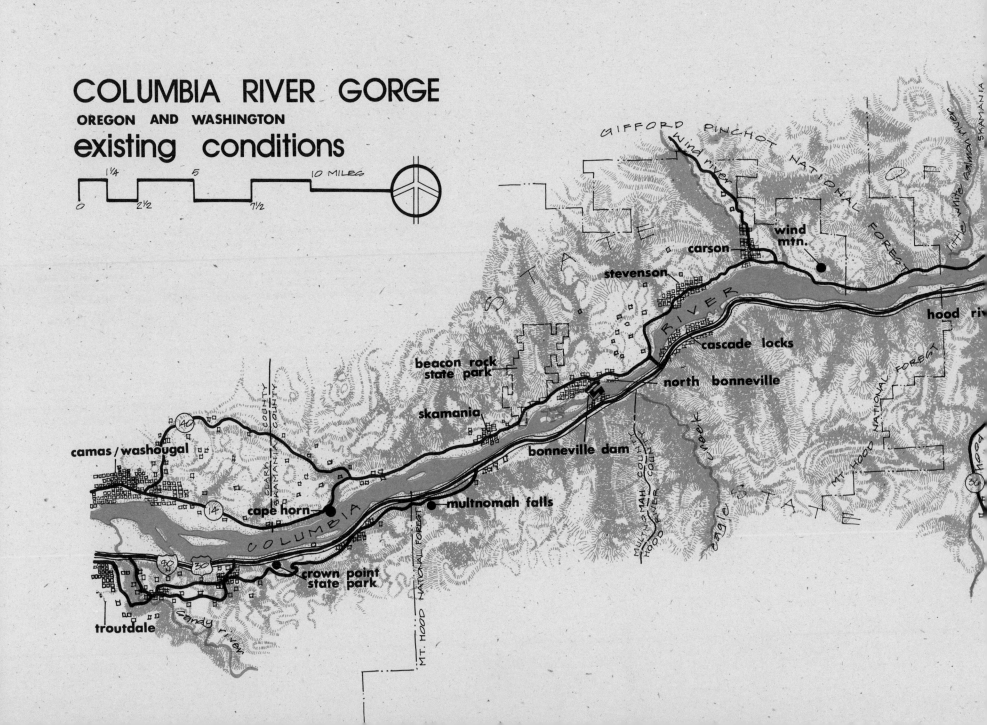

COLUMBIA RIVER GORGE

OREGON AND WASHINGTON

existing conditions

0   1¼   2½   5   7½   10 MILES

GIFFORD PINCHOT NATIONAL FOREST

wind river

little white salmon river

white salmon

wind mtn.

carson

stevenson

COLUMBIA RIVER

hood riv

cascade locks

beacon rock state park

north bonneville

skamania

bonneville dam

camas/washougal

cape horn

multnomah falls

COLUMBIA

crown point state park

troutdale

Sandy river

eagle creek

Tanner creek

CLARK COUNTY

SKAMANIA COUNTY

MULTNOMAH COUNTY

HOOD RIVER COUN

MT. HOOD NATIONAL FOREST

MT. HOOD NATIONAL FOREST

STATE